PASSAGES

PASSAGES

HOW READING THE BIBLE

IN A YEAR WILL CHANGE

EVERYTHING FOR YOU

BRIAN HARDIN

ZONDERVAN®

ZONDERVAN.com/
AUTHORTRACKER
follow your favorite authors

ZONDERVAN

Passages
Copyright © 2011 by Brian Hardin

This title is also available as a Zondervan ebook.
Visit www.zondervan.com/ebooks.

This title is also available in a Zondervan audio edition.
Visit www.zondervan.fm.

Requests for information should be addressed to:

Zondervan, *Grand Rapids, Michigan 49530*

Library of Congress Cataloging-in-Publication Data

Hardin, Brian.
    Passages : how reading the Bible in a year will change everything for you /
Brian Hardin.
       p.   cm.
    ISBN 978-0-310-32919-0 (softcover)
    1. Bible—Reading. I. Title.
    BS617.H35 2011
    220.6—dc23   2011025041

Any Internet addresses (websites, blogs, etc.) and telephone numbers in this book are
offered as a resource. They are not intended in any way to be or imply an endorsement
by Zondervan, nor does Zondervan vouch for the content of these sites and numbers
for the life of this book.

Published in association with the literary agency of Daniel Literary Group, LLC, 1701
Kingsbury Drive, Suite 100, Nashville, TN 37215.

Cover design: Curt Diepenhorst
Cover photography: Matthias Clamer / Getty Images®
Interior design: Beth Shagene

Printed in the United States of America

11 12 13 14 15 16 /DCI/ 22 21 20 19 18 17 16 15 14 13 12 11 10 9 8 7 6 5 4 3 2 1

In honor of my father, the Rev. Ed Hardin,
who set the bar high
and lived a life worthy of the prize
of the upward call of God in Christ Jesus.
His shoes are too big to fill,
but his footprints will indeed be followed.

CONTENTS

ACKNOWLEDGMENTS

To write a book requires great commitment, much refinement, and a generous amount of encouragement. Although authors have something inside they want to say, it is not easy to give it voice, and it takes a community of people to actually get the job done. With that said, I would like to acknowledge the following:

Jesus. You are the inspiration. Life will never be the same because you simply refused to stop pursuing my heart.

My wife, Jill, has been on my journey every step of the way as I have been on hers. Together we share the adventure of life. In Yiddish there is the word, "Bashert." It means that it was meant to be — that one has found a soulmate. Not everyone finds his or hers. I did.

My children, Tyler, Cristian, China, and Maxwell, have been the greatest of my gifts from God. The stories I tell in this book are stories of transformation from one person to another because of Scripture. I was a very driven and selfish person in pursuit of his own kingdom in younger days. Nothing shows a man the patience and love of the heavenly Father found in the Bible like the love one has for his children. I am blessed beyond what I deserve.

The Rev. Edward and Rosalie Hardin made this possible

through their love and commitment to one another. Although my father has passed, my mom remains a constant reminder of what grace looks like in the world. I owe most everything to the goodness of my parents.

My brother Jaymey is a strong man of character and has inspired and encouraged me throughout my life. I send my love to him and his wife, Lindsay.

My friend Brad Mathias has been a comrade born for the battle for the last decade.

My friend Rob Tate has been one of the most stalwartly loyal people I have ever known.

The Daily Audio Bible team is an integral part of my day-to-day life now. Those of you who have so willingly given yourselves to this mission are truly loved. In particular I thank our moderators, Tara, Leslie, Debbie, Tom, Kellie, and Bonnie. I thank my assistant and community engagement guru, SarahJane. Nobody coordinates like SJ. Thanks to our mission's directors, Mike and Jennifer Greenberg (and I should say that Mike has been an irreplaceable part of the team in getting the word out about this book and the Daily Audio Bible in general). Thanks to our techies, Chet and Rob, and everyone who remains unspoken here. I'd need to write tens of thousands of names down to thank everyone because we've done something for which there were no manuals; we created a community wrapped around the globe that feels more like a family than anything else.

Thanks to the Four Winds Mission and WindFarm Café community. You are the localized grounding to all of this. The journey has been made more complete because of you. I love you. I'll fight for you as you've fought for me. Community is something that must be contended for, and in this you have done well, my brothers and sisters.

There are a few people who have been mentors and truly

influential people in my life either by their books or by their actual presence in my life. They number too many to count, but a few cannot go unmentioned. The Rev. Dale Evrist, who was my pastor for seventeen years and remains a true father in the faith to me, made me want to be a godly man. The first mentor I ever had in the creative arts was Bernard Terry. I could never have developed these gifts without his encouragement and faith. The writings of John Eldredge and the friendship of the Ransomed Heart team have been irreplaceable. I've been mentored from afar by these men, and I must speak their names here in gratitude: John, Craig, Morgan, Bart, and Alex. Thank you for modeling community and going after the hearts of men and women all over the world. My heart is fully alive because of your toil.

My heartfelt gratitude goes to the team at Zondervan and my literary agent, Greg. Thank you, Angela Scheff, for originally believing in this project and for the first edit. Thank you, Sandy Vander Zicht, for personally taking the manuscript from something good to something great with masterful skill and for seeing that these words were worth saying. Thank you, Amy Ballor, for your work on editing what I'd spoken aloud into words that could be read on the printed page on the Bible portion of this project. Thank you, Tom Dean, for your marketing skill. Thank you, Jackie Aldridge, for fighting to get the story told. Thank you, Verlyn Verbrugge, for the final touches and words of great encouragement.

Finally, thank you for reading this. My deepest joy would be that this book gives you the desire for a relationship with the Bible. I believe if followers of Jesus would commit themselves to the daily counsel of the Bible, there is little that can't be done. May we move ever closer to that day.

Brian Hardin

CHAPTER 1

THE OLIVE COUCH

And this is the sound of the underground.
Of history in the making, foundations shaking . . .
this is the sound of the underground.

—Pete Grieg, *The Vision*

Choose today whom you will serve.

—Joshua

fell onto my olive-colored couch. After years of friendship, it cradled my body intimately. The house was silent and I was about to force a crisis of faith. I'd prayed the New Year's Eve prayer again nine months earlier — the one about somehow forging a deeper relationship with God and the obligatory commitment to read more of the Bible this year. I remember asking Jesus, somewhat sarcastically, if there was any way I could honestly draw closer to him without someone having to die. It's easy to hold onto Christ when there's nothing else to hold onto. It's more difficult to hang onto faith when things are fine. Somehow this prayer found its way past a crack in the ceiling and floated up to heaven because there I sat at the end of myself, with real choices staring at me like a loaded revolver. Change had been blowing in with the summer breeze and now I had to choose.

My father had been a minister for thirty years, so I grew up under "the shadow of the Almighty." Christianity had been such a part of my life I couldn't really see the world any other way. I didn't know how to. My childhood was spent in a trailer behind a new church every couple of weeks while Dad supported us as a traveling evangelist. My days consisted of home schooling, entering the sanctuary and preaching the previous evening's sermon to the empty pews, and then making a cross in the parking lot with spare wood and crucifying myself with rock nails. I can't remember not knowing Jesus. He was woven into my life at the cellular level, but somehow the faith of a child becomes the faith of a ragged-out workaholic adult.

My folks never really outlined my life for me. They chose moral guidance over rigid authority, figuring I'd find my way. I never got too crazy. It wasn't until my late teens that I declared my independence, so they had to deal with a moody artist and a tough transition into adulthood; but they didn't have to deal with an overabundance of teen angst. I'd found my love early, and although I had my share of broken hearts, music had never failed me.

As an early teen, I could usually be found wearing a pair of headphones listening to anything I could get my hands on. I woke up to music, ate lunch to it, slept it, dreamt it, and started it all over again the next day. By the time I was sixteen, I'd decided that anything short of a career in the music world would be utter failure for me, and I threw out every plan B that had ever occurred to me.

Shortly after that I met a mentor. He just happened to materialize in church one Sunday as if he'd beamed in from the *U.S.S. Enterprise*. I became obsessed with the little demo studio in his basement, and all the minimum wage money I could earn went into recording there. I recorded my first song as a surprise while my parents were away on holiday. Bernard's style of mentoring worked sort of like my parents had reared me. I had to sort it out. I'd come upstairs after cursing the tape machine for not obeying me and ask him what I'd done wrong. He'd smile and say, "I believe if you just think it over carefully, you'll figure it out." I'd walk back down the stairs still cursing under my breath, but he was right. I learned fast and it stuck.

By the time I graduated from high school, I was making money producing records, and the busier I got, the faster life moved. Bernard had a streak of good luck as well. His little eight-track recording studio became the place to be in a matter of months when one of his records sold two million copies. It was off to the races, and I got to watch it from the front row. There was no going back. Within a couple of years I had a manager and the work kept coming. My goal was to pick up one day and survive in Music City, and it wasn't too long before I did.

Christian music and I came of age together. The Christian music industry was struggling to stand up and be something, and I was determined to be a part of it. It was my cause and mission in life to find my way to Nashville, where everything seemed to be congregating. I'd read every issue of any industry magazine I could find.

When I arrived in Nashville a few years later, I was ready. I thought I'd have to do music during the day and deliver pizza at night for a while, but it never happened. Although I was able to work right away, I learned quickly that Nashville was a lot different than the little Michigan city I'd come from. I was the little fish in a sea of world-class talent, and regardless of my mission, there was heavy competition. I put my head down and started plowing and didn't look up for ten years. I didn't look up until I found myself sitting on my couch all but ruined. Had music finally failed me?

The End of the Beginning

The previous year had started like the rest: work hard and then work hard to get more hard work. I'd tossed my New Year's prayer earnestly enough to God, the one about getting closer to him, but I had all but forgotten it by the second week of January. I earnestly wanted to read more of the Bible too. I started sitting in church and reading Scripture, taking careful notes on the things I thought were inconsistent. I thought I'd eventually get through the whole Bible and present this document to God so that he might defend himself against my scrutiny.

This was about as far as my commitment went because I'd found my way into the fast track of an emerging company that was buying up the entirety of the independent Christian music landscape. They were spending money like they had it, and I was right at the ground level. It seemed I'd hit the mother lode. Apparently I'd be making records for years to come for these guys. When I was asked to extend myself and complete a couple projects without payment while they got their subsequent rounds of funding in place, I went against my better judgment and continued. Records were completed, turned in, and released, and before I knew it, I had lived a year on my savings.

Things quickly turned south, and I had broken a cardinal rule in the music business: never begin work without a budget check in the bank. I'd broken the rule — and it had about broken me. In a quick maneuver, the upper tier of leadership was shaved off. I was asked to step in and try to work with the team to salvage the company's burning carcass. I didn't have a choice. All my money was at stake. If it didn't survive, I assumed I wouldn't either.

For eight months I worked eighty-plus hours a week trying to turn the ship. The one bright spot was Red Bull, cigar smoke, and a fledgling friendship with a kindred soul forged in the fire of stress. Brad and I took barrage after barrage of heavy artillery as I tried to create low-cost product while he juggled how we would get it to market. Everyone on the team worked their hearts out, but in the end it was too far gone. We started late and failed. I walked out of that office building in Franklin, Tennessee, knowing that as soon as the owners filed the bankruptcy papers, my life savings were gone.

So I sat in an empty house, alone with nothing left but a friendly couch and a few painful decisions. I found it ironic that my choices were matters of the heart rather than business maneuvers. All I'd known for eight months were business maneuvers with a thin veneer of faith over the top in hopes that God would bless the effort. Psalm 127:1 says, "Unless the LORD builds the house, the builders labor in vain." This was a defining truth, and it created the fulcrum on which my life was delicately balanced.

I considered the poverty of the semi-agnostic life I'd been living. Let's be honest: Isn't that pretty much how many of us live as Western Christians? We acknowledge God and possibly even go to church regularly. Perhaps we even donate generously. But when push comes to shove, what kind of spiritual foundation do we really have? I had little. There was a little boy with the faith of a warrior in mothballs locked away in the attic of my heart, but now as a father with little boys of my own, my faith was anemic and my existence was balanced on a frail ledge. To say I was a good spiritual leader for my wife and children would be like calling Billy the Kid a good pastor to his band of outlaws.

I couldn't deal with it anymore. The kingdom I'd built had just tumbled before my eyes in a matter of months. I considered atheism. I thought about forgetting faith and finding solace in not having to deal with a moral compass of any sort other than what would serve me. I considered picking up a vice or two and jumping back into the fray. I'd just kill or be killed because that's what it felt like my life had boiled down to. "It's nothing personal; it's just business" were the poisonous words I'd heard one too many times. But behind door number two was the chance to give faith a fair play. No holds barred. An all-expenses-paid, one-way ride to absolute surrender.

Sitting there on that couch, the choice stared me in the face. It was one of those true existential moments, and in the end, I chose to honor my heritage and actually give faith a genuine effort from my heart. I vividly remember the prayer. It wasn't a sinner's prayer, and it wasn't eloquent. "Jesus, I'm done with the crap. I'm finished. If you want me to go to Des Moines and make hamburgers for a living, I'll pack up our stuff tomorrow and leave. I'm fine with that." It felt as if I was standing at the edge of a precipice looking out over waves of the vast unknown. What I was contemplating was jumping.

"I'm going to believe that you're nearby and that you can seize me before I hit the bottom," I prayed. "If you don't, I'm dead. I believe my heart will die, and I fear it will be the last time I care about anything."

I jumped — and in the falling, I finally understood that as much as I needed to live by faith, I also needed to surrender my identity. For years I had been trapped in believing that *what I did* was *who I was*. This free fall gave me the oddest sense of release. In that leap of faith, who I was and what I did separated, and my sense of self was stripped clean.

I'd like to say the burden lifted and a ray of sunshine came through the window accompanied by the scent of fresh lavender, but it didn't happen like that. I was utterly numb. It was one of the only times I felt perfectly at peace with whatever might come next. Then the phone rang. I was offered immediate work for immediate cash. Grocery money. Then another call and an email. Monthly bills. Provision never stopped after that, but that's only the beginning of the story.

The Bible and the Epiphany

In the flames of hardship as I thrashed about to save what I thought was my sense of identity and financial security, I had started to read the Bible every day. My friend Brad and I were traveling so much in the end that I had gotten into the habit of reading it aloud to him in the car. Now that was over. I had now chosen sincerely to give faith an honest place in my life, and I found I missed the Scriptures. I missed the rhythm of reading them. They had become a source of comfort to me. I can't confess to giant leaps of spiritual growth during that time. All I can really own up to is trying to pilfer a little consolation for my frayed nerves while trying to look clean and pretty for Jesus so he'd save me in the midst of my trials.

In spite of this, something was happening to me on the inside, and when I ceased exposing myself to the words contained in the Scriptures, I knew something was different. The bizarre piece of this equation is that I wasn't reading the Bible to gain deep insights into the mystical regions of the soul. I wasn't trying to solve theological quandaries either. I was just reading it for what it said, and often it said something that got stuck in a corner of my mind and loitered there for days.

Stuff like, "The person who plants selfishness, ignoring the needs of others — ignoring God! — harvests a crop of weeds. All he'll have to show for his life is weeds! But the one who plants in response to God, letting God's Spirit do the growth work in him, harvests a crop of real life, eternal life" (Galatians 6:7 – 8 MSG). This was my life right there on the page, echoing prophetically over a couple millennia. It not only contextualized what I'd been experiencing; it gave me a north star and a measure of hope that I couldn't rationalize but I couldn't deny either.

When I removed the Bible from my routine for a few days, I started to feel vacant; but as the equilibrium returned to my life, I found the old struggles returning. These weren't struggles of faith. My faith was steadfast. When I made the choice to take the leap, the tectonic plates of my soul shifted. "I choose to believe" has been my mantra since that day in the face of doubt.

The struggle was for time. I began to rationalize that I was reading something I didn't really understand anyway. When I would take the time to read the Bible, the calm would return, and sure enough something would invariably leap off the page that I'd never understood. I knew a lot of the Bible. I could quote Scripture. But I'd never read the Bible in context, and the more I did, the more fascinating it became. Soon it was less about footprint poems and promise verses and more about a story that was unfolding. It was less about extreme customs and animal sacrifices and more about the epic story of God. I started seeing things that I could relate to in spite of the cultural differences. I began to find my own face staring back at me from the pages.

Podcast

In October 2005 I was working on a lengthy design job. I'd expired the battery on my iPod and I remembered reading about an emerging technology called podcasting. I did a quick Google search and in a few minutes I was listening to a guy driving home from his job just verbally trashing everyone around him. It was hideous, but a flicker of possibility began to glow in the back of my mind. I searched more and located podcasts that were seriously making a go of it in the underground world. They were funny and engaging in an indie sort of way that I hadn't heard in a long time. This was grassroots, and I thought it could be a revolutionary marketing tool for the music world. Little did I know that the core plates of my life were about to shift again, and this time I was about to experience a sudden and immediate change of direction.

One morning during the second week of December 2005, I awoke after a restful sleep to a message that was apparently waiting for me to open my eyes. "I want you to podcast the Bible," it whispered. I sat up, shook off the dream, and made a pot of coffee. "I want you to podcast the Bible" became the tape playing over and over in my subconscious. I thought it was one of the more stupid things to get stuck there. First, I didn't know anything about podcasting other than how to listen to one. Second, I had no time for something like that. And third, I had been generally comfortable being a behind-the-scenes sort of guy. Podcasting the Bible would be completely against the natural order of my life.

"I want you to podcast the Bible" played on. After several days, I finally sat down and asked, "Jesus?" Bingo. A bona fide directive from the Lord delivered in a way that rang true to my heart and was an instruction to do something I would never, ever have done on my own. My willingness to move all our stuff to Des Moines and make hamburgers wandered back into mind. I sighed deeply. "Okay."

As I started preparing, I noticed that this burgeoning technology had little help for a regular person. You had to have some geek credentials hidden behind your front pocket penholder to offer a podcast, but somehow I managed to sort it out enough to put my first recording on the Internet by Christmas. I told cyberspace that I had no idea what I was doing and that I had no idea who might come into contact with the message, but that I was planning to start reading the Bible every single day starting on January 1, 2006, and hopefully I would get all the way through it by the end of the year, one day at a time.

The premise was simple enough for me. I was going to just do what I'd been doing. I was going to read the Bible every day in a good meal-sized portion and process it in context. I was finding that the Bible was making more and more sense to me as I digested it in chapters rather than random verses. I thought I'd just flip on a microphone, read a chunk, and react to it just like a normal person.

By this time I thought God was pulling a practical joke on me. Part of me thought the whole thing would get called off. I'd get a blue star on my obedience sheet, and a more qualified person would step up. Another part thought this was how God was finally going to get me through the Bible. By the end of the year I expected there might be five people who would sign on to go through it too, and we'd be Internet pals and sort of hold each other accountable. This is how I would tell my grandkids about how I came to read the whole Bible.

These were incorrect assumptions.

By the time January 1 rolled around, 257 people had emailed to say they'd be joining me. By June, the Daily Audio Bible podcast had been downloaded 200,000 times. As I write these words, the number has exceeded forty million downloads reaching every corner of the globe.

There was a strength building in me along with a battle. I'd sworn to myself that I would never be a minister and never be in ministry. I'd watched up close and personal the cost of those sorts of activities. My father remains the most ethical and godly man I've ever known, but I grew up with the keen awareness of what Christians are capable of doing

to each other. This whole notion of never being in ministry was being challenged by the day as emails of averted
suicides and restored relationships started appearing in my
inbox. The Bible was working almost like magic — almost
like it promised to. I'd shake my head at some of the things
people were saying to me and look skyward and ask once
more, "Why am I the guy? There are more qualified people
for this, you know."

As my spiritual life continued to grow, my exterior world
was beginning to fray. My commitment to the Bible was
taking a toll on the well-worn habits of my life. My plans
and the agreement that I'd made with myself about avoiding
ministry were starting to come apart at the seams. By July
of 2006, I nearly had a meltdown. I was so fantastically irked
that God had asked me to do this, I couldn't see straight.

Yes, there was genuine spiritual fruit coming from the
effort. The calls and emails of lives being changed continued
to mount, and many of them reduced me to tears. But the
stress level and the sense of battle surrounding the ministry
was taking me out. I was already as busy as any two men,
and to produce a quality podcast every single day, seven
days a week had pulled forty full days out of my schedule. I
didn't think it was fair. I was begging for relief.

It was then that I realized forty days was about a tenth
of my year. It was an epiphany. I might be willing to give
cash to the cause of Christ, but I was desperately holding
onto my time. When I got my head wrapped around the
fact that I'd been inadvertently holding out on God what I
thought was most precious to me, I began to carve out time
in my life like a front-end loader clearing a field for construction. I assumed that I would simply hold on and finish
well; December 31 would be a day of celebration and libera-
tion. I would have read the Bible all the way through — and I

would be done with it. I'd replay the reading on the Internet and quietly frolic off into yonder fields.

Again, I was incorrect.

September rolled around, and I began to sense deeply a community developing around the Daily Audio Bible. I began to see people shouldering the loads of those they'd never met in regions of the world they'd never visited. I saw people confessing things that would get them crucified were they to bring them up in their local church. I began to realize that God wasn't asking me to read through the Bible once and then check it off my things-to-do-before-you-die list. This was to be a way of life for me.

The community was full of people who had been wounded in one way or another by religion but were not willing to give up on God. It was full of losers trying to find hope. It was full of seekers looking for the truth. It was full of people who felt they were unwelcome in church. It began to dawn on me that even though I'd sworn I'd never be in ministry, the identity that had fallen away was now being transformed. I was being invited into ministry, and I was passionate about it.

Passion and Irony

When I was a kid, I used to sit in church and listen to missionaries tell of distant Africa or the dangers of China with a twinkle in their eye and a slideshow to prove they'd been there. Like most of my friends, I cringed at the idea. It actually made me *not* want to pray too much or get overly serious for fear God might ask me to live in a hut and drink water that people did their laundry and perhaps other business in. I talked to my father about this. His advice was that I really didn't need to worry about such things because if God were inviting me to Africa, I'd begin to feel a passion about it that would grow until I couldn't think about anything else. This was a big relief because all I could think about was music and girls, two subjects I was passionate about, so I felt that being a rock star would be my rightful calling.

The irony is my father was exactly right. My friendship with the Bible has taken me the scenic route from who I was to who I was created to be. My path began with an act of obedience to read the Bible every day, and it wound its way almost backward to the beginning, forcing me to deal with the stresses and compulsions of trying to carve out an identity that was mine alone with God relegated to a back-up plan. It took me back to the wounds that life can bring and invited me to compare what they were saying about me with what God was declaring over me.

The Bible isn't hocus pocus and reading it doesn't give you magical powers, but it does reveal to you who you really are and illumines a path that you were created to walk. When I began to believe its words and obey its instructions, life began to align with what it said, and this has made all the difference. My heart has been transformed completely. I find myself passionate about things that previously seemed drudgery. The neon blinking lights of culture do not seduce me as they once did. I have little use for the plastic life that makes many promises but rarely delivers on anything at all.

The apostle Paul said, "I have learned to be content whatever the circumstances. I know what it is to be in need, and I know what it is to have plenty. I have learned the secret of being content in any and every situation, whether well fed or hungry, whether living in plenty or in want. I can do all this through him who gives me strength" (Philippians 4:11 – 13). This pretty much sums up what the Bible seems to do to us when we allow it access to the deeper places in our lives. The discontent aligns with God's will, the broken heart is healed, the chaos of the world fades to a distant drone, and life becomes vibrant because there is a reason to live beyond the next paycheck.

When I completed my first full revolution through the Bible, I recall looking in the mirror and realizing that I didn't see anything the same. The realization hit me that I had been unwittingly transformed from the inside out, and I looked at just about everything through different eyes. I looked at God differently; I looked at my wife in a new way; I saw my role as the head of my home from a much more sobering point of view; my need for community was solidified — everything had changed inside of a year.

I began throwing out the challenge to the Daily Audio Bible community that I am tossing to you now. If you will commit yourself to spending every day in the Bible for one month, you will notice something shifting inside. If you'll do it for three months, you'll feel as if major places in your heart are coming back to life. If you'll stick to it for a year, you will have been transformed from the inside out.

I've read through the Bible in large portions seven days a week for well over two thousand days consecutively. The man that I was is no longer here. I don't look at the world the same in any way. I liken this to working out at the gym. If you stick with it a month, you begin to feel healthy. Sweat it out for a quarter of a year and new lines of lean muscle begin to appear. Hang with it for a year and you'll have a new body and the energy to go along with it. Our hearts seem to work the same way. I'm inviting you to the adventure, and I am quite certain that if you expose yourself to the Scriptures every day for a while, there is no way for you to remain the same.

CHAPTER 2

WHY DON'T WE READ THE BIBLE?

———————

I am a creature of a day. I am a spirit come from God, and returning to God. I want to know one thing: the way to heaven. God himself has condescended to teach me the way. He has written it down in a book. Oh, give me that book! At any price give me the book of God. Let me be a man of one book.

— John Wesley

I am here but my heart's in Iceland.

Heart's In Iceland
— The Obvious

A few years ago I found myself wandering around New Mexico. I was driving across the country, and in Albuquerque I decided to head southwest and onto lonely roads in the general direction of southern California. I'm fond of the desert, and New Mexico offers some professional grade isolation. Two hours out, I noticed a massive saucer in the distance. It's hard to judge how far away things are in the desert because it's so vast and expansive. You think you're a couple miles from something and fifteen minutes later you still have twenty minutes to go. The dish turned into two, three, and four, and pretty soon I could see a line of them. I had wandered into the National Radio Astronomy Observatory and its Very Large Array system. Twenty-seven dishes spanning twenty-two miles across the desert floor were looking to the sky for answers.

Answers. These little puzzle pieces that get placed on the kitchen table of life and eventually emerge into a mosaic of truth. And the truth is what serves as the foundation of our lives. Without it we crack in minutes. We have no compass, no North Star, and we are virtually blind in our pursuit of direction.

What I hope is that we find some answers — and that we fall in love. You may have never considered the Bible in terms like these before, but I'm hoping you can put aside your assumptions for a few hours and dream. What may have seemed a chore or obligation in the past could actually become a dear friend and in many cases will be the clear voice of direction to you. Scripture can be your intimate ally and your close confidante when chaos swirls everywhere else in your lives.

This is the very Word of God. What we need for the life we were created to live is contained within its chambers. This Word is a lamp to our feet, and in the dark it will light our path (Psalm 119:105).

In the gospel of Matthew, Jesus tells a story: "The kingdom of heaven is like treasure hidden in a field. When a man found it, he hid it again, and then in his joy went and sold all he had and bought that field" (Matthew 13:44). This is the reality of the Bible. It offers us a complete change of paradigm that leads to authentic freedom. But it won't come according to our predefined terms or assumptions, and it most definitely won't fit into the folder of life we call spirituality. It's an all-consuming proposition, much like the man who sold all he had to purchase the field that contained the treasure; but it's the only way out of the madness.

Most people believe the Bible is the truth. According to a recent Gallup poll, 78 percent of Americans believe the Bible is the Word of God.[1] That's about 230 million people in the United States alone. About 67 percent of Americans say that the Bible holds the answer to the basic questions of life,[2] and yet only one in seven spend any extended time in Bible study.[3] Even though we claim to need it, we avoid it with every distraction and entanglement we can twist our way into. Where is the disconnect? Why don't we read the Bible if we believe it is God's Word and contains the answers to life's questions? We can be such strange creatures.

The irony is that as believers we actually *want* to read the Bible. So why don't we? There are the obvious distractions.

Time is always an enemy. Reading Scripture is always on our perpetual to-do list; but as the day goes by, it ends up at the bottom of the list, and by the time we fall into bed, we're just too exhausted to read anything that requires serious thought. Understandability also seems to rank high. In fact, the Catholic News Service reports that more than half the people surveyed in Europe and North America say the Bible is difficult to understand.[4]

There is no shortage of excuses. But if we're honest, we feel a little guilty that we're not reading the Bible because the framework for our life is supposed to be built on it. How could something so important seem to mean so little? The ironies compound themselves because we want to have a better relationship with God, we believe the Bible is the truth, and we believe it contains answers for our lives, yet reading the Bible is the one thing we continue to ignore.

There's a sobering reality lurking just beneath the surface, one we probably wouldn't say out loud. Maybe we don't really believe reading the Bible will work for us. We've claimed to place our hope in it, but we also keep our expectations in check. We're leery this might be the spiritual equivalent of an infomercial diet plan guaranteed to give us a ripped body with little or no effort. But as exciting as it might sound, it's probably not going to work. Maybe it will work for really spiritual people like pastors and missionaries, but not for us. The problem is that this line of thinking makes confetti of the faith we thought we had.

But maybe it's time. Maybe unraveling the layers of life and what we thought we believed will lead us to what we've been searching for all along: the truth, a foundation, a holy context for life.

◼

Back to my trip. A little south of the Very Large Array site the road abruptly became unpaved. I realized I was now on roads I'd seen from the air that seem to go on forever but end nowhere. Two hours later, I started seeing trees. Trees that were not on the map. Trees that were not supposed to be in the desert. I couldn't turn around and get anywhere near civilization quicker than the route I was already on, but I didn't know yet the fix I was in.

The road had deteriorated into a washboard full of potholes. I had to cling to the steering wheel to keep from knocking myself unconscious on the roof of the car. I had to slow down to fifteen miles per hour, but I had no choice but to continue. This was now the only road available. Darkness was descending, and it started to snow. Pangs of worry gnawed at the back of my mind. I had no idea things were going to become so challenging, and I certainly didn't know that New Mexico ever got snow.

I rounded a bend and got a brief glimpse of my altitude. I'd been climbing in the forest, and when I came into a clearing, I realized I was higher than the highest Appalachian peak back East. The snow was now blowing in earnest on the exposed pass. Fear challenged me to a duel, and several minutes later, it came back for another round.

I had come upon a running creek about twenty feet wide, and the road went down and through it. No bridge. I put the car in park and exited the vehicle to judge my chances. I could see it was quite shallow, but the climb out on the other side was steep and icy. I drove into the water whispering silent prayers and was greatly relieved to come through the water and up onto the path on the other side.

Doesn't this sort of resemble our everyday lives? Aren't we constantly finding ourselves in the unknown where every choice leads to a predicament? The job is uncertain and the economy isn't giving it any help. The education so long fought for is funneling into a life far less passionate than it seemed at the start. The marriage is speeding alarmingly in the wrong direction. The kids simply will not stop doing everything they can to kill each other. Life is passing by. This was not the plan, and all the while it looks less and less familiar.

Wouldn't it be comforting to have just one friend who actually knew what was going on, who would always tell the truth and not be afraid to tell it like it is? Don't we long for the kind of intimacy that would cheer us on without pandering, that would hold our hand even to the fire if we needed it, that would laugh deeply, cry honestly, and stay true? Wouldn't it be like finding treasure in a field? We do have such a comrade — the Bible.

It's time to abandon the limitations we've placed on the Bible. It contains the sacred words most people believe are inspired by the one who gives us our very breath. How have we lost sight of this? And how can we ever come into a trusting and intimate relationship with the God of Scripture when we feel so conflicted about Scripture itself? How do we make sense of a book that seems to offer passion, love, and hope, but simultaneously remains mysterious and somehow foreign?

This is a peculiar conundrum, and yet isn't this the way our lives happen? Weren't all of these feelings intertwined the first time we made love to our spouse? Don't we experience both serenity and tension in the relationships that mean the most to us? We can receive unexpected bad news and suddenly no longer recognize our own reflection in the mirror. We can also experience joy that radiates to the very core of our beings — and these experiences can both happen on the same day. Doesn't life unfold full of drama and seemingly contradictory experiences?

The Bible is written as a story, a story that has not yet reached its conclusion. The story has wound its way through battlefields and wedding nights, through birthing chambers and funeral parlors, from transcendent pleasure to utter hopelessness. The story has come through voices around Bedouin campfires to stone tablets, from the skins of animals to the printing press. It has passed through ages long forgotten to ages dark and forgettable. Its echoes bound from enlightenments to reformations. This is the unstoppable story of God and his profound love for humanity.

You are a part of this story. Your ancestors and heroes are contained within these pages. This is our story. To become intimate with the Bible is to finally find ourselves. To understand that the stage is set and we have a role to play in God's story is finally to come home. We must completely wipe away our suppositions and shift our orientation. Once we do, we will begin to see with the eyes of our hearts the way we were meant to. We've grown a long way in other directions, but we must return to where we experience God, our hearts.

So often we attempt to approach the Bible from a purely intellectual perspective and forget that Christ actually dwells in our hearts. Shifting our orientation makes all the difference. The Bible is an unfolding story in which we have a role; it's not a series of facts and principles that, if followed meticulously, will yield a desired result.

If we return to the beginning of God's story, we see a garden with two trees. One offers life; the other, knowledge of good and evil. A man and a woman are there, and the woman is chatting with a serpent. The serpent calls into question whether or not God has told them the complete truth, and then he offers an alternative reality through the forbidden fruit. When Eve ate and gave Adam a slice, a trade was made—life for knowledge. This is such a sad scene, and yet it explains so much.

In the beginning there was no need for a mosaic of answers placed on the kitchen table of our experiences. The human race actually had the truth. We had God perfectly. Our curiosity about what we might be missing has repeatedly been our undoing for ages beyond recollection. Isn't it interesting that in the garden before the fall, Adam and Eve would actually have needed to have faith in the possibility of sin, death, separation from God, and hardship? They had no knowledge of such things. They had an intimate friendship with God. This is how our lives were supposed to be. This is how we were created.

■

The snow was coming hard and the ground was completely covered save two muddy tracks supposedly for tires. Darkness had settled in, and I was becoming more and more frightened. I rounded a curve that banked sharply right before a very steep climb, but I never got there. I indeed rounded the bend and began the climb when my wheels started to spin and I commenced sliding backward and sideways. My eyesight went white, my heart went boom, my outer extremities went numb, and I cried out with a loud voice—but I didn't say, "Jesus," as I probably should have.

I decided the best thing to do was to remain calm and just breathe and think. I got out of the car and flicked on a tiny flashlight from my camera bag. Backing up and trying to turn around was not an option. I could slide right off the side of the road. I wouldn't fall to my death, but I would be entrenched in a snow embankment ten feet or more down until the spring thaw. Moving forward didn't look promising either, but to even attempt it, I had to extricate myself from a snow bank. But I had left my snow shovel and salt back home, and all I could improvise to shovel my way out was with a plastic CD case. I went at it for about five minutes, realizing with heightening anxiety that I would not be digging out this way. Not in the dark — and probably not in the light either.

I had almost resolved myself to spending a solitary and fearful night on the mountain when out of the corner of my eye I thought I saw a flash of red, and then it was gone. I sat very still and watched for it. Nothing. Five minutes passed. Nothing. I was beginning to think the anxiety was causing strange psychological things to happen to me — and then I saw it again. I waited. Sure enough, there it was. Up on the mountain about half a mile was what appeared to be tail-lights. I got out of the car and headed in that direction. As I stumbled up the slope, I realized there was no way I'd make it across this pass in a car. The snow was nearly a foot deep.

I could see the lights were, in fact, taillights, and they were attached to a big pickup truck. Another man-sized truck was in front of it and a horse trailer was sitting unhitched to the right, with a horse stoically staring at me uninterested. I saw four pair of cowboy hats and four sets of steamed breath backlit by spotlights from the lead truck. It appeared I was about to walk into the company of real living cowboys.

There was a part of me that wanted to fall at their feet and plead for mercy. But there was also my pride that wanted to walk into the middle of the bunch and say, "Howdy!" — as if getting stuck on the side of a mountain in a rental car was something I did at night for pleasure. I went with authenticity and meekly told them I'd gotten myself stuck and wondered if they could pass along a little advice. One cowboy looked at me and said, "Go on back to the car and we'll come 'n' git ya." Twenty minutes later, I slid into the passenger seat while one of the cowboys took the reins. The man-sized pickup backed down, and they chained me up.

"You go ahead and sit tight over there. We're gonna need to get some thrust going to get us all across," he understated. We flew up the side of that hill and across the pass in a white knuckled blitzkrieg to safety. I wasn't able to manage even a whimper. When he got to the part about sending me on my way, he gave me an earful of mouth about staying off these mountains unless it was summer.

"This north face doesn't get much sun so there's snow most of the time. You're up at ten thousand feet. You want to be careful, son." Another understatement. "If we hadn't been here, you might have met with a different version of your fate."

Those words echo and replay in my mind as I consider life without Christ. They haunt me when I consider the bleakness of an existence without the counsel of Scripture. This is our predicament: we're wandering on perilous roads in a world fraught with danger. There's an Evil One, and were his wishes exposed, they would reveal our untimely and unsavory end (1 Peter 5:8). We're high on a mountain in the blinding snow, but we've convinced ourselves through distractions, addictions, and busyness that we're actually on a path leading somewhere. In the deepest parts of the evening, though, while we lie in bed trying to stare past the ceiling to the heavens above, we feel the emptiness of it all. When the facades of life have turned off their neon sign for the evening and all is still, we feel the hunger of our deepest soul crying out for nourishment, but we simply don't know where to begin.

We start making a checklist.

1. Get in shape. If I got in shape, I'd feel better about myself.

2. Get more culture. If I understood the world better, I'd be a better person and could help more people.

3. Get organized. If things were a little more in order, life would feel more manageable.

On and on it goes. The irony, as we lie in the dark, is that likely within arm's reach is the answer. It's the red taillights just up ahead. It's the offer of rescue. It's the hope of our salvation. The Bible is sitting there like a perfect gentleman awaiting our arrival. When we reach out, it will come and pull us over the pass to safety, and it will lead us on the paths to life (Psalm 16:11).

A word of counsel: when you reach out, be prepared. You're embarking on the adventure of a lifetime. It's the treasure in the field, and it will ask you to joyfully let go of all your entanglements to lay hold of it (Matthew 13:44). It will expose the hidden motives of your life (Hebrews 4:12). It will debunk the false and institute the true. It will take you the scenic route, for walking with God is not about efficiency; it's about love.

Remember when you were dating? Those long walks to nowhere? Going out in the rain and splashing until you were soaked? Ordering a sundae and sharing the same spoon? None of this was efficient, but did you ever feel so full and complete? Didn't time seem to stand still? Didn't time seem not to matter?

This is where the Bible will take you because this is where God is. He desires to share his world with you, but that will mean making room for an authentic relationship with him. You'll have to fight for it, but as you do, you'll begin to realize that so much of what you've been up to are things that you don't really want in your life anyway. The Bible will reveal what is really going on and where you fit in.

Moreover, it's sobering, because you have a role to play and it's irreplaceable. It will call out your noble heart and ask you to rise up. Your value cannot be calculated. When you complete your first revolution through the Bible, you'll feel as if you've woken up for the first time. The world will not look the same. Your revolution through the Scriptures will have been nothing less than a revolution in your life.

This isn't hocus pocus. I'm not promising a problem-free, unopposed life. When you know the truth, the puzzle of life makes sense, for you no longer have to make the pieces fit in a solitary attempt to make life work. You have the wisdom of the ages and the counsel of your Creator now. Things are about to change, and there's no going back. But trust me; you won't want to.

CHAPTER 3

THE BENEFITS AND BLESSINGS OF READING SCRIPTURE

We must be careful with our lives, for Christ's sake, because it would seem that they are the only lives we are going to have in this puzzling and perilous world, and so they are very precious and what we do with them matters enormously.

— Frederick Buechner

Change me. I can feel the way you're slowly taking over.
    God, I will surrender.
I'm throwing up my hands now to the One who saves me.
You give hope so freely. Here I am, invade me.
    Fill me with your change.

"Change"
— Sherry Muchira[5]

What if we do read the Bible every day? What's supposed to happen? What can we really expect? I can say with all honesty that *everything will change*. But it may not be the way that you'd think. Change will happen from the inside out, not the outside in. If you're thinking about reading the Bible as something to check off your list of things to do, you may miss it completely. If you're looking for a genie in a bottle, you will be disappointed. The Bible isn't a magic book of ancient wisdom; it's a book about life and about God's love for you.

It's going to be nearly impossible for you to interact with the Bible on a daily basis for the next year and walk away unchanged, but the change will come in profound and unexpected ways, for you are embarking on an adventure, not reading a manual. Your problems aren't going to vanish, but they will no longer have a hold on you. You're probably not going to make a million dollars by the end of the year, but you will be content and thriving. All the stresses of life aren't going to disappear, but there will be a sense of serenity that somehow transcends the normal chaos. The world will not spin slower, but some of the superfluous things will lose their appeal.

My husband and I always spent time with the Bible each weekday morning, but on the weekends we were often distracted by kids and other priorities. We tried to get time in after dinner or sometime in the afternoon, sometimes before bed. Those days just ended up bad. We argued more, had poor attitudes, resorted to sarcasm. Then one weekend when everything started going south again, we finally questioned what the difference was between the weekdays and weekends. We realized that we hadn't focused on Scripture or prayer at the beginning of our day. So, we changed our habits and started focusing on God's Word seven days a week and wow ... so much more peace! It sounds almost "magical," but it really isn't; it is just making God the priority, making him the center. It has made a huge difference in our lives.

—Sheila, from Dallas, Oregon

The Bible will challenge you to reorient your life to God and will offer you the life you were created to live—which may not be the life you are currently in. What you'll find is the utter relief of truly trusting God and finally believing that although his ways are beyond us, he actually knows what he's doing. He really does love us, is present, and wants authentic life to be our everyday experience.

There are many benefits and blessings that come out of an intimate friendship with the Bible and walking with God on a daily basis. While this chapter isn't designed to be an exhaustive review of *all* the Bible offers, it will highlight a few important ones to widen your horizon.

Hope

When I read the Bible every day I feel I am getting to know God better. The words I read are healing to me, I feel peaceful, and God has worked more powerfully in my life. When I started to read God's Word every day, I had a wonderful breakthrough in my marriage. I have also felt free to express myself, and the Holy Spirit has freed me tremendously by getting rid of pent-up emotion. I've never wailed and cried so much. It's been amazing.

—Jane, from Lincolnshire, UK

It's pouring. It's been like this for three days. The sky has descended and hovers just beyond reach but feels oppressive enough to have a personality and thick enough to slice. There is none of the drama that often accompanies the southern skies when storms blow in. All is a sullen and constant grey. The sun has set the past couple of evenings with no trace of its brilliance. I wouldn't have even known it set except that the sky turned from grey to slate to charcoal. This evening, however, is different. Far off on the horizon is a thin red line, and it reminds me of why we trudge on through life. Hope. That little red line brings with it the promise of a widening blue sky and the warmth of the sun again.

Hope is what we hold onto when life descends on us like a grey cloud, when the blur of responsibility and obligation make every day look the same, and when the future doesn't seem to promise anything that the past hasn't already given. Hope is the flicker in the dark when the abundant life in Christ we'd been counting on seems just out of reach and weariness threatens to capsize us. Hope is one of the greatest blessings that the Scriptures give us: "There is surely a future hope for you, and your hope will not be cut off" (Proverbs 23:18). This confident expectation of things to come encircles our hearts and protects what remains tender and vulnerable.

The Bible offers us a baseline for hope. It also gives us a reason to hope beyond ourselves because it reveals how interconnected we are, not only with everyone around us but also with the story that's been told for thousands of years. Scripture's plumb line that provides us a straight and narrow path through life is irreplaceable — especially when we've lost our own internal coordinates and connection to life. "Hope deferred makes the heart sick, but a longing fulfilled is a tree of life" (Proverbs 13:12). This we know to be utterly true. The irony is in the verse that follows: "Whoever scorns instruction will pay for it, but whoever respects a command is rewarded."

It's vital that we not only know certain verses that can provide comfort but that we allow the Bible to unfold and guide us in the way it's meant to. We can't just make it into a sound bite because doing that doesn't lead us into the richness of its texture and into the life it speaks of. If we want to live in the hope that Scripture offers, we need to engage it deeply and in context. We need to see the Bible as an intimate friend and receive its guidance as from a trusted ally.

As with all relationships, this requires something of us. True to its nature, the Bible isn't going to provide some incantation that we can whisper or some promise that if memorized and recited a thousand times a week will change everything like magic. It will undoubtedly force us to rethink a number of priorities and convictions, and it will force to the surface the very things that are stealing our hope and robbing our joy. It will flood them in the revealing light of truth and force us to make some decisions. The beautiful thing about having a loving friend like the Bible is that although the decisions and choices may be difficult, they will also be clear, and in making them we will be entering into the rest the Bible promises.

I experienced this kind of rest and companionship with the Bible when I faced a difficult career decision. Any vocational change is stressful, but leaving a career I loved to pursue something I'd previously vowed never to do made the transition especially intense. The decision to leave the music business and pursue vocational ministry hasn't been easy, but the choice to do so was clear. In the process, I had to wrestle with difficult questions about the impact I wanted my life to have. After spending time in the counsel of Scripture, I realized that most of what I'd been doing made no contribution to how I wanted to be remembered.

I was especially impacted by what the apostle Paul wrote in his letter to the Galatians, "But the fruit of the Spirit is love, joy, peace, forbearance, kindness, goodness, faithfulness, gentleness and self-control. Against such things there is no law" (Galatians 5:22 – 23). I knew that I was not experiencing these things in the life and work I had in the music industry, which meant my life was not a fruitful one. But I could easily see the fruit of the ministry God was inviting me into. I knew that pursuing vocational ministry put the trajectory of my life in alignment with Scripture, and I felt the deep and unexplainable sense of peace. Although I was walking away from the only career I'd ever known and loved, I had a clear sense that vocational ministry was what I was supposed to do. Being obedient has its benefits.

When you are clear about what God wants you to do, it takes the guesswork out of difficult decisions. After living this out for several years, I've developed a passion to love God and to be obedient to his Word. If I'm doing that, regardless of what the circumstances may be, the rest isn't my problem. Knowing this, I've experienced great freedom and hope even when life is difficult.

Peace

In April of 2006 I was diagnosed as having a serious heart problem. It took a few months before doctors decided to do open heart surgery, and the days between April and August were very difficult. I am no stranger to hardship. I lost my brother and both my parents [when I was] between the ages of 15 and 26. I also had a daughter who was born with spina bifida. In all the things I had gone through, God had been faithful to me. It was difficult, though, lying in bed at night when my heart felt like it was pounding through my chest and anxiety tried to creep in. I began to read the Bible in earnest. There were many nights when I barely slept at all, but the Scriptures comforted me.

—Randall, from California

Life can descend into insanity pretty quickly. The kids are in a bad mood before school and won't cooperate, so we resort to yelling at them and feel a cloud of guilt all day that permits just about everything to go wrong. A call from the boss changes our hoped-for weekend plans. The car breaks down in the driveway, our teenager is on the warpath again, the toilet is backed up, and our toddler is playing in it. Each day brings with it the promise of sunshine, but we're always expecting to be thrust into a downpour without an umbrella.

What if God's Word could actually bring a change of weather to our exhausted souls? What if chaos could be escalating all around us, but we were able to deal with it systematically without being carried off in the torrent? What if the insanity of life could be around us but not in us? The prophet Isaiah tells us, "You will keep in perfect peace those whose minds are steadfast, because they trust in you" (Isaiah 26:3).

The promise of peace is a thread that winds its way throughout Scripture. The comfort we find in knowing that we are not alone is often the only thing we've got to hold onto, and yet this offer of peace goes well beyond our current circumstance. It encompasses the whole of life. The apostle Paul in his letter to the Philippians says:

> Rejoice in the Lord always. I will say it again: Rejoice! Let your gentleness be evident to all. The Lord is near. Do not be anxious about anything, but in every situation, by prayer and petition, with thanksgiving, present your requests to God. And the peace of God, which transcends all understanding, will guard your hearts and your minds in Christ Jesus. (Philippians 4:4–7)

Peace is an enormous benefit to our lives when it's present, but it's one of the hardest things to hold onto in a world that moves so fast and demands so much of us. Yet Scripture does promise us transcendent peace in spite of it all. How do we get it and keep it?

As we enter into an intimate friendship with the Bible, we'll find rather quickly that it becomes our daily tutor and biggest cheerleader. It lovingly instructs us, but it also requires us to know what it's telling us and to do what it says. The apostle Paul tells us that in order to participate in the offer of peace, we must trust God, fix our thoughts on him, rejoice, be considerate in all we do, remember that the Lord is coming soon, don't worry about anything, pray about everything, tell God what we need, and thank him for all he's done. It's only after these instructions that we get to the payoff. Then we will experience God's peace, which exceeds anything we can understand (Philippians 4:4 – 9).

The Bible promises us much, but it requires that we begin the process of reorienting our lives to the lifestyle it requires. Only by enjoying the Bible in an intentional and spacious chunk of time that allows us to absorb and reflect what it says do we begin to fully appreciate its message. This leads us to a conundrum. It's awfully hard to force one more thing into our day, and it doesn't take long with the Bible to realize that it's not going to sit at our feet begging for a place in our lives. It's more like a lover playing hard to get — it longs to be pursued. The Bible will intrigue us, and the more time we offer, the deeper it will draw us into the relationship.

Any relationship built to last must first of all be built. Most relationships that reveal and offer everything there is without the element of mystery, character, and time may indeed be passionate, but they will burn out quickly, leaving a charred shell of what could have been. The Bible isn't going to be any different. We cannot dive in, grab what we want or need, and then leave. These are the words of life. They are the revealed Word of God, and they offer the pathway to intimacy with God. The Bible isn't something to be used for our own needs. The Bible is about orienting our lives to God and thereby getting all the nourishment our souls require.

One trip through the Old Testament in context will reveal just how passionate God is and how deeply he feels about us. He first lovingly and meticulously creates a perfect world, carefully crafts humankind in his image, and breathes into them his own breath of life. God offers his heart to the people he created and makes himself vulnerable to their free choice. Humanity's decision to opt out of perfection deeply wounds the heart of God, but he constantly pursues a covenantal relationship. From Abraham to Isaac and Jacob and to Joseph he offers rescue and safety to his people. Through Moses, he frees them from slavery and establishes a new culture in the desert. Through Joshua he brings them into a land flowing with milk and honey that they may live in peace and tranquility. It's as if he's brought them back to a sort of Eden again; yet humankind once again rejects his love.

Through the prophets Ezekiel and Hosea God speaks eloquently as a discarded lover, but his passion and profound love for his people is so perfect that he will not give up. It's like he's standing outside the hotel room door while the one whom he loves gives himself or herself to another lover. He can hear the illicit act taking place through the walls. It's deeply painful, and yet he waits for them to emerge not so that he can exact revenge, but so that he can tell them that his love will not fail.

One trip through the New Testament will reveal the great lengths to which God has gone to in order to win our hearts. Under the cover of poverty, homelessness, and scandal God incarnate comes as a baby. In order for humankind to be fully restored to God, justice must be served, and the cost is beyond humanity's ability to pay. So God in the flesh, in the person of Jesus, models what life can and should look like. He teaches us how to love and how to live, and in the end he once again demonstrates the unspeakable and unknowable depths of his love for us.

As Jesus is being fixed by spikes to an executioner's beam,

he cries out in unbearable physical pain; yet intermingled with these gasps of anguish are words of forgiveness for the men who are killing him. This forgiveness extends far beyond his Roman executioners to all of humankind. Jesus came to model life and then to lay down his own so that what was lost at the beginning could be restored and offered freely to all who will believe.

We long for many things, but there is little we seek more sincerely than deep and abiding peace. The Scriptures do indeed promise this very thing, but God will not force it on us. This may seem strange, but God has given us what the seventeenth-century mathematician, physicist, and philosopher Blaise Pascal calls the "dignity of causality." In other words, God has provided us with a free will. We get to choose, and our choices matter.

Although God is just, holy, righteous, and fiercely wonderful, he is also respectful. The Bible demonstrates the great lengths God will go to in order to offer us things like peace, but he will not invade our personal space to force it on us. Rather, he offers us his Word and invites us to walk with him.

It's in the reaching, tugging, and tearing ourselves away from the things that bind us to a life that is less than what he offers that we actually find the peace we're longing for. There is simply no way to get from here to there without allowing the counsel of the Scriptures free rein in our lives. It's not so much that we cannot find time to cram one more thing into our lives; it's that anything that prohibits the Word of God from having its proper place in our lives must go. This is not only the pathway to peace; it's the secret of Scripture.

Think of it like this. If you're taking a class and faithfully studying from week to week, when final exam time comes you will be well prepared not only with what you need to know in order to pass the class but also with lasting knowledge of the topic you studied. However, if you wait until the day before the exam to crack a book, you'll be full of stress and anxiety. What little information you manage to cram into your brain may help you answer a few questions, but you won't retain it once the test is done. When it comes to experiencing peace, we can't cram it in at the last minute; we need to build a foundation for it by giving God's Word a central place in our lives.

Correction, Guidance, and Self-Discipline

Over the last five years, God has been dealing with me about self-centeredness. In that time I retired from my job as a geologist and finally began to understand that he wanted 100 percent of me. He wanted more than just what was left over from my great career and hobbies. I began to learn that he was Lord and King of my life and to bow my knee to him. I've learned to lay the "crown of the kingdom of Russ" at his feet.

I began to spend daily time in the Bible in a way I never had before. As I've soaked in it daily for the past three years, it's been part of what God has used to speak his mind and will into my life, and I've finally surrendered in a way I never did in the previous thirty years.

Time and time again God has confirmed that he wants all of me, not part of me. I've learned I need to be 100 percent in or out — no in between. I am certainly still in that process, but he is using his Word to show me how he cares for me, wants life for me, is seeking a total relationship with me, and has nothing but my best in mind if I will but listen and obey.

—Russ, from Urbana, Illinois

The Bible blesses us with correction and guidance externally and internally. Externally it invites us, of our own volition, to embrace it, ponder and meditate on it, and ultimately live it. Avoiding these things is actually the largest obstacle standing between us and what our hearts long for, but once we overcome it, a vista opens and the possibilities become endless.

We're starting to clue in to the fact that we really must make room in our lives for God's Word if we want what God's Word offers. We're also well aware that carving space in our lives to jump off the never-ending treadmill of responsibility and obligation and then to devote that time to peaceful contemplation and study isn't the simplest thing to sort out.

I used to ponder these things each year sometime in late January after my New Year's resolutions wore off. That's when I typically began the process of rationalizing how I didn't have time for the Bible and how it just didn't seem to be doing anything for me. Ironically, I'd simultaneously be justifying the end of my New Year's exercise program. *There's just not enough time. It's too hard. I hate the gym, I hate waking up early to read, I'm just not seeing the results I was so pumped up about a month ago, and if I eat another bland chicken breast or read another genealogy I'm going to puke.* So I'd give up. Soon the time I'd set aside for the Bible filled up with frantic activity. I'd wake up in the morning, enjoy a cup of coffee, and attack the day, not stopping until I laid my head down on the pillow that night, exhausted.

In those twilight moments before sleep crept over me, I'd stare at the ceiling feeling that there must be more to life. I'd realize with a tinge of hopelessness that although I'd been utterly consumed with activity during the day, none of it really mattered. I was busy, but few of the activities that consumed my time were things I was truly passionate about and almost none had any eternal value. Over time, I began to realize that not having time for the Bible was actually a willful decision on my part, and in making that decision I was actually choosing to live a life I didn't really want.

The Bible functions like a signpost signaling a constant fork in the road. To continue on the spiritual journey, we are forced to make a choice between the proverbial wide and narrow roads. The wide road is the well-traveled one, the path of least resistance in which we feel guilty for not reading the Bible but fail to make a place for it in our lives. This sense of guilt is actually our heart's lament that we're settling for much less than we should be. The Bible invites us instead to choose the narrow road, the only pathway that leads to the truest part of who we are in God. It's an opportunity to choose a life well lived, but it is a *choice* — God does not coerce our decision. By an act of our own free will we must surrender to it, and in doing so we'll find freedom and release.

Internally, the Bible guides and instructs us by providing a framework for living the life God wants us to have. In his pastoral letter to his protégé Timothy, the apostle Paul wrote, "All Scripture is God-breathed and is useful for teaching, rebuking, correcting and training in righteousness, so that the servant of God may be thoroughly equipped for every good work" (2 Timothy 3:16 – 17). This is precisely what the Bible does. It offers us continual instruction that is readily available for whatever we're facing at any moment.

It provides the wise guidance we desperately need when life feels more like driving in a winter whiteout than breezing down a summer highway. Once we begin to experience just how vital and relevant the Scriptures are to our daily lives, we don't want to engage any important decision without its counsel. This is as it should be, because the Bible is the Word of God, the counsel of our Creator.

If we were offered the opportunity to sit down with any person throughout history who had made an incredible impact on the world, we'd jump at the chance. Maybe we'd sit in a café with King Solomon and question him on the ways of wisdom, or perhaps we'd select Beethoven or Michelangelo and glean from them the intricacies of creating art that moves people for centuries. Given the opportunity, we'd cancel whatever we planned in order to speak with these people, and we would think nothing of it. The Bible offers us the opportunity to sit with the Lord of heaven and earth, who speaks and creates from nothing! This opportunity is given freely and is available always, and yet we complain about not having time for it.

This settled over me one evening as I got ready for bed, exhausted from another day of endless activity. Something clicked, and I finally realized that the one true and eternal God wanted personal time with me. But instead of being honored and awed by God's desire to be with me, I treated him like a distraction or a nuisance. It occurred to me that I was rushing by God as I had sometimes rushed by musicians who hung out in the lobby trying to get my attention — as if God was trying to hand me a demo tape that I knew I'd never listen to. It was a painful realization and I knew immediately that something was terribly askew. I felt embarrassed and ashamed, and I knew I needed to cancel or move whatever seemed pressing in order to make time for the wisdom of the ages.

Life

I grew up in and am still part of an amazing Christian family and church community. I came to God very young, and I have always felt loved and protected by God. As a child, my innocent faith experienced many answered prayers; I believed absolutely anything was possible. My biggest challenge was trying to have a personal relationship with Jesus. A young child trusts and believes that there isn't anything a parent can't do, but at the same time, the child doesn't fully understand a parent's heart; it's something that comes later.

This is what I feel the Bible has done for me. By spending time with it every day—hearing about God in the Old Testament and about Jesus in the New and a bit of wisdom in between—I am finding I know the heart of God more fully. It's as if I feel pain for the things that hurt God and joy and excitement for the things that please him. I feel that I have a God perspective I didn't have before.

—Sharon, from Belfast, Northern Ireland

In John 15 Jesus uses the metaphor that he is the vine and we are the branches. He breaks it down in simple terms by telling us that life is not going to work apart from him. If we remain in him, he will remain in us, and that connection will bring life. There is no possibility of true life outside of this connection, for without him we can do nothing. When we invest our precious energy in crisis management instead of applying it toward our relationship with God, we're always going to end up with frayed nerves and a head full of confusion.

The vine and branches Jesus is describing is the life flow of our relationship with him. A branch gets its nourishment from the vine or trunk. Our spiritual nourishment comes from Scripture, which provides the context for a dynamic relationship with God. This isn't just religious jargon thrown in for encouragement. Our relationship with God is informed by Scripture, and according to Jesus this relationship is what gives us life itself.

If, for some reason, one of our fingers were to get lopped off and was sitting on the table next to the rest of our hand, we can certainly try to will the finger to move. We can use all the reflexes and muscle impulses that would have normally moved the finger, but it's no longer attached. It's not getting the signal. It's not going to move. It no longer has life in it. This is our fate if we remain disconnected from the lifeblood of Scripture.

It's likely that we're already aware of this both intuitively and in reality because we've undoubtedly experienced what life (or the lack of it) looks like apart from Jesus. By contrast, however, if we are connected to the vine, we have an enormous amount of authority bestowed on us to engage the promises and lifestyle the Bible offers. The Bible tells us the truth about who we are (see John 1:12; Romans 5:1; 1 Corinthians 6:17; Ephesians 3:12; Philippians 3:20; and Colossians 2:10, for starters).

We are all seeking life. It's built into our DNA. Every commercial offers it and every romance novel, every magazine article, and every toy we buy promises to give it to us. Sometimes we settle for counterfeits such as materialism, an addiction, or any other obsession; but in the end, everything fails to give us what we want. The entire book of Ecclesiastes is a study on the meaninglessness of life without God, written from the perspective of a man who had seen and done it all. King Solomon had over a thousand of the world's most beautiful women waiting for his call. He had riches and honor that brought dignitaries from far and wide just to observe it; his wisdom and cunning were feared and revered. From an earthly perspective, his exploits are still referred to thousands of years later. Yet, in the end, he found it to be meaningless. All of his pleasures and pursuits did not bring life.

What Solomon sought — and what we all seek — is authentic life. Jesus said, "The thief comes only to steal and kill and destroy; I have come that they may have life, and have it to the full" (John 10:10). Full and abundant life, Jesus says, is the very reason he came. This life cannot be found in earthly pursuits alone. King Solomon, the wisest man ever known, demonstrates this. Jesus, God in flesh, demonstrates this.

When we expect external things to bring us peace and happiness, we live our lives backward — outside in rather than inside out. Living from the inside out correctly orients us to the vine, the life force of God within us. From this place of connectedness we experience the abundance we crave. And when we have an insatiable desire for more of God, we are truly living an authentic life.

Just as our bodies need a balanced diet, our souls require a steady diet of Scripture. There's no way to circumvent this process. We can decide, for example, that we no longer want to eat protein, but our bodies will suffer the consequences. In order to be healthy, bodies require the sustenance provided by high-nutrient foods. In the same way, the spirit within us cannot survive without the Word of God. God sets us a banquet. He offers us 31,173 nutrient-rich verses about himself and encourages us to feast! Inexplicably, we choose to fast instead. That's what happens when we slide into the misguided notion that we can enjoy a life of faith without routinely consuming God's Word. It won't work.

On the other hand, we nourish our hungry souls when we devote a balanced and generous amount of time to feasting on the truths of Scripture. It doesn't take long to notice the change. The Bible is life-giving — it revives every famished heart and breathes resurrection power into deathbed souls.

Maturity

Two months after I had a beautiful baby girl I lost my mother to cancer. Then we had to move in with my father in order to take care of him. I got a job with a company that repeatedly failed to make payroll and then the whole economic crisis hit. Life was a real struggle and my heart was so dry and hard all the time. I hadn't spent much time in the Bible up to that point, but now I am gradually seeing God's Word soften my heart and guide my focus back to him. These changes have been so visible that my husband and family members have made positive comments about them.

Where I live it is not a wise choice to publicly announce your faith in Jesus, but since I have made my faith public in my workplace, I feel such freedom. This is all a result of God's Word being a part of my life! The Bible says that God's Word never returns empty. This is true, and it is changing my life.

—Khulan, from Mongolia

In his book *Creation in Christ,* George MacDonald writes, "What father is not pleased with the first tottering attempt of his little one to walk? What father would be satisfied with anything but the manly step of the full-grown son?" This is one of the tensions we experience in life. We desire to be full-grown people of faith, but we don't always relish the idea of the work it takes to grow. Somehow we must come to grips with the fact that we will never run the race of faith until we first do the strength-building work of learning to walk. It doesn't work in the physical world, and it most certainly will not work in the spiritual one.

The apostle John celebrates the fact that we're all in differing stages of development, but those stages do build on each other (1 John 2). The point isn't to dwell on how weak or immature we are currently; it's that we're all in process, and our goal is to become fully grown and mature persons.

The apostle Peter said it like this, "Like newborn babies, crave pure spiritual milk, so that you may grow up in your salvation, now that you have tasted that the Lord is good" (1 Peter 2:2 – 3). The pure spiritual milk Peter refers to can only be attained through Scripture. Our heavenly Father loves us as we love our own children, and he longs for us to mature just as we desire growth and maturity for our own sons and daughters. He doesn't want us to stagnate; in fact, if we've entrusted our lives to his care, he won't allow it. It's not healthy for us. It would be profoundly unloving to allow us to remain weak and feeble.

In his letter to scattered Jewish believers, James provides a key insight about how God brings us to maturity. He writes, "Consider it pure joy, my brothers and sisters, whenever you face trials of many kinds, because you know that the testing of your faith produces perseverance. Let perseverance finish its work so that you may be mature and complete, not lacking anything" (James 1:2–4). James's point is this: rather than allowing our troubles to overwhelm us, we can embrace whatever we're facing, knowing that we've not been abandoned, the challenge will not last forever, and it will inevitably bring about maturity in our lives.

The apostle Paul affirms this truth: "God works for the good of those who love him, who have been called according to his purpose" (Romans 8:28). Chaos loses its power to derail life when we can see it as more than just a problem or hardship to be overcome. When we have the clarity that God redeems everything for our good, circumstance fades into the background, and God takes his rightful place at the center of our lives. Everything we face in life can be (and is being) used to increase our strength, endurance, and trust in God. And everything is in the process of being redeemed and converted for our ultimate benefit. This is how we teach our own children to grow, and this is how our heavenly Father is with us.

A Friend with Endless Benefits

Hope, peace, guidance, life, maturity. These are but a few of the many benefits and blessings that come as a result of a friendship with the Bible. Much could be written about things like wisdom, freedom from fear, strength, or healing and restoration. The truth is that the benefits of immersing ourselves in Scripture could easily be a book in and of itself, but even that would still be inadequate. Trying to cover the vast scope of Scripture's impact is to try to cover the totality of life itself — and this is impossible.

What King Solomon said of the proverbs he wrote holds true for all of Scripture. They are

for gaining wisdom and instruction,
   for understanding words of insight;
for receiving instruction in prudent behavior,
   doing what is right and just and fair;
for giving prudence to those who are simple,
   knowledge and discretion to the young.

                         (Proverbs 1:2 – 4)

  The benefits and blessings of reading Scripture in a nutshell are a better life for you, your loved ones, and the world. When life is properly oriented to God and lived from a place of trust, it becomes far less about limitations and much more about possibilities.

    When engaged on a daily basis, the wisdom and counsel of Scripture become the whispers of our Creator, guiding, directing, and loving us into every benefit and blessing that life with him brings. We were created to live a perfect and perfectly balanced life. We gave that up long ago, but God hasn't given up on our total restoration. The Bible is the guide.

CHAPTER 4

HOW THE BIBLE WAS MEANT TO BE READ

Tell me the stories that fill your life
and I will tell you who you are.

— Unknown

That you are here — that life exists, and identity;
That the powerful play goes on,
and you will contribute a verse.

— Walt Whitman

Why is it so hard to read the Bible? I mean, we want to. At least somewhere inside we think we'd like to. We like the idea of it, but when we crack open the big book, we're lost. We have no real context for it, and randomly opening to a page and throwing down our finger hoping for a mystical revelation doesn't usually work well. Then there's this constant low-grade guilt that eats away at the back of our minds. We feel like we must be failing as good Christians because we simply don't understand the Bible, and we can't find the time to figure out how to approach it. It's supposed to speak to us and guide us, but once we get beyond the verses we memorized in Sunday school, we're simply lost. How do we actually get anything out of Bible study?

If we're going to attempt an answer, we must put away the idea that the Bible is a rule book we're supposed to measure up to or that it's so cryptic we need a Master of Theology degree to unlock it. Conversely, it's not a book full of dainty little promises from a God who more resembles Santa Claus than the Lord Almighty.

The Bible is a book about life. Our lives don't come to us in prepackaged bites, and neither does the Bible. How many times have you opened your day planner and watched everything you'd planned fly out the window by noon? Proverbs says, "In their hearts humans plan the course, but the LORD establishes their steps" (16:9). Each day is a new adventure whether we like it or not. We might have a general outline of what we'd like our day to look like, but we rarely know what might come sailing in on the breeze. Life comes at us in drama, intrigue, and emotion. Life comes to us as a story.

The Story of Life

Imagine we're the best of friends, and we haven't seen each other for awhile. We both happen to be in town and finally are able to schedule dinner. What will we talk about? More than likely we'll catch each other up on our lives by telling stories. We'll laugh at a funny one and cry over a sad one. Stories contain within them all the emotion and sensory expressions of life. It's how life is lived and how we communicate.

We must approach the Bible as a story — the story of God and of God's people throughout history. What makes it dynamic and present today is that the story hasn't ended. We're each a part of the living, breathing story of God's passionate relationship with humankind, and we each have a place in it.

If you're retelling the event about how a coworker spilled coffee all over her white blouse and her embarrassment at her dainties showing through and the only words you use for the entire recollection are, "There was no paper towel in the supply closet," how will I know what you're talking about or have any context for it? Similarly, if you randomly read a verse of Scripture without knowing what the story is about, you'll have no idea what is being communicated.

You may know the old joke about the man who was looking for guidance and threw his finger down on these words: "And Judas went away and hanged himself" (Matthew 27:5) — without knowing the story; he had no idea why a hanging was being discussed in Scripture, much less a self-hanging. This man was looking for God to speak and came across this verse out of context. What do you imagine he assumed the Bible was saying? He sensed that he'd accidentally selected the wrong page, so he flipped again and threw his finger down on Luke 10:37, where it says, "Go and do likewise." Now what? He was feeling sort of low when he came to the Bible for comfort and hoped God might speak, but he wasn't really thinking about hanging himself, and yet the Bible was seemingly telling him to do just that.

The Bible must be absorbed in the context of story just as life must be absorbed and processed in the context of its events and outcomes. Understanding that the Bible is a story about God and his heroic love for his people allows us to approach it with a little more context for the adventure we're about to embark on.

Transferring the Treasure

The biblical narratives were first communicated orally by nomadic people. Around evening campfires, wide-eyed children listened to the stories of God's creation as each nightfall brought the wandering community back together. Abraham's travels around the Fertile Crescent were originally recounted not in a temple but beneath a desert sky. When God promised Abraham that his children would outnumber the stars in the heavens, it meant something concrete to these travelers.

From the earliest ages, youngsters were taught the traditions and belief in the God of Abraham, Isaac, and Jacob, but they were more than just campfire tales. These oral recitations were given word for word precisely as they'd been handed down from the generation before. Children memorized them and became the keepers of the customs and rituals as each new generation emerged. Telling and retelling the sacred story was ingrained into their culture and woven into the fabric of their lives. Each story was recounted in its entirety. They didn't simply grab one line of narrative such as, "Go ... to the land I will show you" (Genesis 12:1) and mesh it with something else. To this day Jewish culture has the written Torah (Old Testament) and the Talmud — an oral tradition that expounds on the written Torah and is believed to be inspired by God and given orally to Moses.

We get a sense of the nomadic lifestyle of the early patriarchs and begin to understand the context in which these stories were handed down as we read the story of the lives of Abraham and his progeny, known as the children of Israel. The first five books of the Bible are known as the Pentateuch and are traditionally considered the writings of Moses. By the time Moses takes the stage, the children of Israel are enslaved in Egypt. We get the benefit of front-row seating to God's creation of a culture, a culture that deeply influences us today. Moses is thought to have been one of the first people to chronicle the oral histories into written form. From this point on, the written Word appears. This was the Bible of early Israel.

As we watch God free his people from the bonds of slavery in breathtakingly epic fashion, we also see the importance of story. It seems important to God that his children do not forget what he's done. Throughout the Old Testament, God instructs people to build an altar or a pile of rocks to mark the spot where something significant happened. It wasn't so much that he wanted a quick sacrifice and worship session; rather, he didn't want his people to forget the importance of what had taken place there. In the same way that the traditions were passed on orally, God instructed those who witnessed his awesome power to leave a concrete reminder of what he had done for each generation to come.

When we hold a Bible in our hands, we are holding the ultimate reminder. The Bible is what has been written about God's glory, power, and consuming love so that every generation for all time will not forget. When we begin to see it for what it is, the Bible quickly becomes a sacred heritage in which we all have a part. We can find ourselves in its pages.

By his own finger, God wrote on tablets of stone and delivered them to Moses. That which is written in stone remains forever, and it is from this event that we get the saying "written in stone." The law given to Moses was a lasting set of convictions, rules, and governing ordinances written in stone. They were not to be deviated from, nor were they ever to be forgotten. This was the Bible in its entirety at that point in history, and God's instructions set a precedent that continues throughout all Scripture. Remembering and adhering to these commands were so important to God that he insisted every king who ever ruled Israel must sit down and make his own copy of the written Word in its entirety in front of a priest (Deuteronomy 17:18).

Constant study of and adherence to the Scriptures was a mandate for God's people. The king was instructed to always keep his copy with him and read it daily as long as he lived. This was how he learned to fear and obey the Lord. This daily interaction with Scripture as a command has never been repealed. The law "is to be with him, and he is to read it all the days of his life so that he may learn to revere the LORD his God and follow carefully all the words of this law and these decrees and not consider himself better than his fellow Israelites and turn from the law to the right or to the left. Then he and his descendants will reign a long time over his kingdom in Israel" (Deuteronomy 17:19–20).

Moses established this sensibility and constantly admonished the Israelites in every way possible always to hear, speak, and consider the words of the Lord. This wasn't a new concept. For centuries, the oral traditions had been passed along through constant repetition. Just prior to his death, Moses gathered the entire congregation of Israel to him. More than a million faces spread out across the desert floor close to the banks of the Jordan River. They were on the verge of taking hold of the Promised Land foretold by God to Abraham.

Moses' parting words in Deuteronomy recounted where they'd come from and reminded them that if they hoped to get to where they were going, they must never forget the Word of the Lord. They must never let it pass from their memory. They must never abandon what God had ordained. After Moses died, Joshua became the leader, and he continued to remind the Israelites of their story. In remembering the Word of the Lord, they could remember who they were.

> Be strong and very courageous. Be careful to obey all the law my servant Moses gave you; do not turn from it to the right or to the left, that you may be successful wherever you go. Keep this Book of the Law always on your lips; meditate on it day and night, so that you may be careful to do everything written in it. Then you will be prosperous and successful. Have I not commanded you? Be strong and courageous. Do not be afraid; do not be discouraged, for the LORD your God will be with you wherever you go. (Joshua 1:7–9)

From the beginning of God's communication with humankind, the Word of God has been held not only in high regard as something holy, but as something that must be remembered, pondered, and reflected on. Joshua instructed the Israelites (and all generations to come) to study it continually and to meditate on it day and night.

Losing Our Place in the Story

If we are honest, this kind of devotion to Scripture is about as far from our experience as Mount Everest is from Death Valley. It's not that we lack desire, and it's only in part that we lack the discipline to make it a priority in our lives. The answer to what has rendered the Bible so irrelevant to our daily lives may lie in the fact that we've lost our place in the story. We've forgotten who we are. We are God's people, and the Bible is the story of us. In many ways, we've lost connection with those who have gone before us, but as the poet Walt Whitman so eloquently put it: "The powerful play goes on, and you will contribute a verse." The narrative that winds its way through Scripture has found its way through time to this very moment, and we who now breathe are smack in the middle of it.

When God decided to invade earth on the largest search and rescue mission in history, it was to redeem his people. We are those people, and yet our experience with God is too often limited to the sinner's prayer, Sunday service, occasional communion, and a higher moral code. Do we really believe that's all that God had in mind?

The Bible is a book of examples, not a book of exceptions. The characters in Scripture are unlikely heroes. Moses was chosen to lead God's people out of slavery, and although he was raised in Egyptian royalty, he became a murderer who was so afraid to speak in front of people that he asked God to send someone else. King David was a mighty warrior and a passionate lover of God, but he was also an adulterer and murderer. In the end, he found redemption and became a man after God's own heart. The apostle Peter was a passionate but impulsive man who sometimes spoke without thinking. Although he was the first to declare that Jesus was the Son of God, he also denied him when the pressure was on. And yet it was on his faith that the church was built.

The Bible isn't devoid of utter humanity and frailty. The heroes and heroines on its pages were all ordinary people who, with God's help, did extraordinary things. All the grit of life is in the Bible because all the grit of humanity is what brings the biblical context to life. Our ancestors in the faith are more like us than like Superman or Wonder Woman. God redeems the human race and invites us on an adventure we can't take on our own. This is the story of the people of the Bible. This is our story.

When it comes to devotion to Scripture, it's instructive to consider the life of Jesus. How did he do what he did? Where did he get such power and wisdom? According to the Gospels, he immersed himself in a deep and abiding intimacy with God. Jesus often eschewed what would seem the most efficient ministry path in order to pray and make space for life.

The Gospels describe how Jesus often rose early to pray. He had become a regional celebrity by this time. The appropriate thing to do would have been to build on the momentum and give the people the show they'd come to see. In one case, the disciples came looking for him because the crowds had arrived. Jesus decided to be a no show. He responded, "Let us go somewhere else" (Mark 1:35–38).

The pressures of life and ministry never stopped for Jesus, yet he took time away to be alone with his disciples (Mark 6:30–31). Although Jesus was compassionate even in the face of exhaustion, he understood and guarded the source of his strength and authority. He consistently removed himself from the fray to create space for God. This wasn't something he did from time to time; this was the continual habit of his life.

Jesus also knew the Scriptures. We find him teaching in the synagogues. The Bible in Jesus' day was the Old Testament, the Torah, and he knew it well. The religious elite constantly tried to trap him with theological questions for which there were no good answers. Jesus' cunning shrewdness filleted their attempts and sent them away red-faced (Mark 12:12 – 17; Luke 20:1 – 8). Lest we consider Jesus' commitments to prayer, time away, and Scripture study an ideal that we have no hope of ever achieving, Jesus himself preempts the argument: "Very truly I tell you, whoever believes in me will do the works I have been doing, and they will do even greater things than these, because I am going to the Father" (John 14:12).

Disconnected Pieces

If we're going to grow into the maturity God has designed us to have, we must modify our thinking. We must begin to think in terms of wholeness, connection, and integration — about the proverbial forest as well as the trees. This is a stark contrast to modern culture, which has us parsing life into small, disconnected elements that we can arrange and rearrange to fit our circumstances. We experience this in the spiritual life when we divide biblical texts into sound bites rather than use the Bible as the baseline authority for life.

This happens in a worship service when preachers observe a truth, back it up with Scriptures taken from various places in the Bible, and then wrap it up into an application-oriented forty-minute talk. This is not a criticism of contemporary church practices. Quite the contrary, God speaks through his leaders both in and out of the pulpit this way. The problem is that this is somewhat of a departure from the way the Bible was read throughout most of history. Rather than viewing the Sunday service as an integrated part of our everyday lives and a celebration of our intimate relationship with God, we've conditioned ourselves to view it as the highlight of our spiritual week or a reprieve from the battles of life. Monday comes around and it's back to the grind, trying to make ends meet while fighting to be good people who have something that resembles a relationship with Jesus. Our prayer life ends up being something we do as we're falling asleep, and Scripture remains the thing we can't find time for.

Think of it like this. Most of us desire nutrition that contains what our bodies need to remain healthy and vital. But the ideal is harder to achieve than the realities of life. Often we find ourselves settling for what we can get at a drive-thru because we've come unprepared to deal with what steals the day. Proper nutrition requires a complete commitment, and it requires the space in life that it takes to plan for and prepare these foods. In truth we have time for whatever we desire the most. If nutrition is nonnegotiable, it will be a reality in our lives. Spiritual nutrition works the exact same way.

As crazy as our calendar can be and as little discretionary time as we feel we have, we are not the first people to have to deal with time pressures. King David, for example, was likely a busy guy. I feel fairly confident that his schedule was as packed as any of ours. He was, after all, the king of Israel, and yet the Psalms are full of songs and poems seeking after intimacy and space with God. As a musician, David put much of his inner monologue to music, and the

Psalms remind us of what is deep inside each of us. King
David writes:

> How can a young person stay on the path of purity?
>> By living according to your word.
> I seek you with all my heart;
>> do not let me stray from your commands.
> I have hidden your word in my heart
>> that I might not sin against you.
> Praise be to you, LORD;
>> teach me your decrees.
> With my lips I recount
>> all the laws that come from your mouth.
> I rejoice in following your statutes
>> as one rejoices in great riches.
> I meditate on your precepts
>> and consider your ways.
> I delight in your decrees;
>> I will not neglect your word. (Psalm 119:9 – 16).

We all long for this to be true of us, but somehow life continues to get the best of our intentions. Perhaps this very fact
is the answer to the whole dilemma. Perhaps we've allowed
the way we prioritize what is most meaningful to us to push
interaction with the Bible to a lower place on the list, a place
we rarely get to.

We sincerely desire a passion for Jesus, and we actually
want an intimate relationship with God's Word, but other
things crowd our space and we buy the lie that we don't
have time to really dig in. We also buy into the lie that Scripture is unapproachable when the reality is that the Bible
holds the keys to so many of life's twists and turns.

The Bible was meant to be read in good-sized pieces —

but more important, the Bible was meant to be read. All of us probably know a variety of promises that the Scriptures offer. Plenty of verses comfort us when we're facing a struggle or encourage us as we take a risk. If we make these verses quaint, one-size-fits-all anecdotes for life's challenges, we'll be plagued by questions about why they don't always work. In effect, what we're doing is treating these snippets of Scripture as incantations or magic spells, which is not how the Bible operates. If we really desire to have the life Christ offers us, we must make reading Scripture in context — with space to breathe — a priority of our life. There's no shortcut on this one.

Jesus said, "Do not store up for yourselves treasures on earth, where moths and vermin destroy, and where thieves break in and steal. But store up for yourselves treasures in heaven, where moths and vermin do not destroy, and where thieves do not break in and steal. For where your treasure is, there your heart will be also" (Matthew 6:19 – 21). These words illuminate the fact that a shift has to take place in our lives. We can't continue to reason that the Bible is something we just can't find time for. The truth is that as believers, *we don't have time to be without it.* If you have read the words of Matthew 6 and find yourself in them, God has just spoken to you through his Word. This is a conversation that never ends.

In order to have the relationship with Scripture that we sincerely desire, we must take a leap of faith and carve out time to breathe it in, to allow God's Word to speak to us. When we take this step, God will invariably show up. It's his Word, but it's our story. After a couple of weeks in the Bible, we'll notice a shift taking place. A couple of months later, places in our hearts begin to unlock. After a year in the Scriptures, we'll look in the mirror and see a different person.

I say this from personal experience. My faith was a mile wide and an inch deep before allowing the Bible to speak into my life. I now feel stable and rooted regardless of what storm is brewing on the horizon. I am not alone. I will not be abandoned, and in the end, no matter what happens, I will be with Jesus.

This is not my experience alone. Millions who have gone before me can attest to this fact. God transforms us from the inside out through his Word. I can't explain that, but I can bear witness to it. It doesn't take long to wonder how we ever lived without it.

CHAPTER 5

LIVING THE BIBLE
IN COMMUNITY

There can be hope only for a society which acts
as one big family, not as many separate ones.

—Anwar Sadat

Never doubt that a small group of
thoughtful citizens can change the world.
Indeed, it is the only thing that ever has.

—Margaret Mead

Better to light one small candle
than to curse the darkness.

—Chinese proverb

School was my ultimate priority and succeeding academically was my greatest source of affirmation and self-worth. I was doing exceedingly well . . . until my success in school began to wane and I crashed. I was left with nothing. I'd shaped my life in such a way that I had no community, no friends, and I generally stayed away from family. I'd grown into such a perfectionist in my life that the way I treated my body, my schedule, my studies, my life, was rigid and controlled (and yet totally out of control). At that time I didn't know Jesus, and I thought that life was something I had to sort out and make work on my own. When I failed at caring for myself, I fell into a very serious depression.

I had reached the end of my wits when one evening I stumbled onto a community of people walking through the Bible together. I was on a desperate search for what I can only describe as "something." These people were genuinely happy, friendly, and loving life. And there I sat, thin and weeping. My heart felt like a black hole and I had nowhere to turn.

Making a connection between one particular group of these "happy people" and their Jesus-freakedness, I searched out the Bible on iTunes. I found the Daily Audio

Bible, loaded it onto my iPod, and began listening. I listened again. Then again, and again. Every day, ten times a day. At school, driving, at home, at work. When I heard the words, I felt a little lighter. The words themselves truly meant nothing to me at first; didn't even make sense to me. How could narratives about animal sacrifices and demands for circumcision somehow bring me peace? And who is this "Son of Man" dude he keeps talking about? It all blurred together; the Old Testament, the New Testament, the Proverbs and Psalms but that didn't matter. Through the Bible, Jesus introduced himself to me, proved himself to me, and I, somewhat resentfully at first, asked him to take control of my life, bitter that I couldn't do it on my own.

The questions I started having from listening to Scripture, paired with a curious sense of relief coming from this book called the Bible, led me to log onto the Daily Audio Bible forums where I knew other people around the world were also listening to the same thing every day in community. People generously and patiently answered my questions. We began praying for one another. I didn't know how to pray, but I did it anyway. I modeled myself after what I saw in others. Every day I'd log in as soon as I got home from school and go to my community lifeline. I'd pray for every single person and talk with people who were now my friends. I was still struggling, still mad at God, still sick in many ways but I was no longer alone.

This tiny group of people has since grown into a huge global community of people a lot like me. New people come every day whose stories aren't so different from mine. In desperation, they also reached out for the Bible. I can't fathom reading the Bible entirely alone. I cannot imagine

> reading it without hearing other people's reactions. I cannot imagine my life without a network of people who share the most vital part of their lives with each other. I know every time I listen to God's Word, I am with so many other people. I just no longer feel alone, ever.
>
> —Tara, Oklahoma City

I began reading the Bible aloud and posting podcasts of it on the Internet beginning January 1, 2006. I thought I was setting myself up for a little accountability so that I'd make it all the way through and finally have context for what the Bible was actually communicating. I had no idea what was about to happen. Almost immediately, a community gathered around it. That community grew so swiftly that within six months men and women of all walks of life and on every continent logged in every day.

As the community grew and took shape and we diligently worked to provide a solid infrastructure for interaction with each other, the whole thing blossomed into a thriving family that crossed every single Christian denomination and tradition as well as every conceivable ethnicity and life story. It's become one of the greatest ecumenical movements of our time. If you peruse the halls of the Daily Audio Bible forums, you'll see a constant conversation taking place about everything imaginable, but the common denominator that provides this unity is the Bible. We've all come to experience Scripture together, and in the daily reading of God's Word, we discover who we are, how God profoundly loves us, and how our lives are supposed to become more and more like Christ. We realized that our depth of love for God is informed by our growing love for one another.

Authentic Community versus Loose Affiliation

Recently as I was watching a football game, one of those catchy beer commercials came on. A good-looking guy is sitting at the bar telling his gorgeous girlfriend about the beer. She looks at him and says, "I've been meaning to tell you something: I love you." He smiles nervously and says, "Well, I lo, I looooerrr, I luuueeewww." He continues struggling to get the words out when the waitress walks by and inquires about another round. He immediately says, "I'd love one."

Thinking about being involved in community can be the same way; we have a hard time making the commitment. Whether we've been hurt before or just want to carve out a vast amount of personal space, we often find ourselves in "loose affiliation" rather than in authentic community. Especially in our Western culture. We like to be lone rangers and show what we can do all by ourselves.

I initially sought out a way to read the Scriptures in community because I had tried multiple times and failed to read through the Bible in a year on my own. Once I started, I realized that committing to reading the Bible in community was more than a personal commitment; it was a commitment to the community as well. We were going to depend on each other. Many of us were on this journey together, seeking to know God more fully, to support and pray for each other.

My life has been enlarged and enriched by reading the Bible in community. I have been especially energized and challenged by thoughtful dialogues with others. It is incredible to experience the impact of Scripture personally and then hear how the same passage impacts people whose life experiences and stories are so different from my own. God never intended for us to journey through a life of faith apart from a community of faith. He has given us the gift of community to enrich our individual lives so our impact on others is multiplied for his glory!

—Bonnie, Illinois

Companies spend billions of dollars appealing to our "army of one" sensibilities. We're made to think that we have no value unless we stand out in a crowd. This isn't the case in other parts of the world. In a familial or community-centric culture, that same car, razor, or shampoo is marketed in a completely different way. The message would tell of what we can do together.

In the West, we cringe when we hear about cultures that have traditions like arranged marriages. We can't fathom the bondage because we believe we're selecting a mate and striking out by ourselves to make a home and family of our very own. We want to create a solitary unit that makes a life for itself and forges an identity separate from other families. In a family-centric culture, however, the marriage is not between only the man and woman; it is the welcoming of a new person to the family itself, and its very survival depends on the right choice. Family identity is what brings value to the individual. Therefore, the families come together, knowing the temperaments and tendencies of the lovers to be and help guide the process to its logical conclusion. These marriages rarely fail.

In many non-Western cultures one's sense of individuality

comes from one's place in a family unit. The family makes its important decisions together because they are literally counting on one another for survival. When a new wife is brought into the family, for example, or a daughter is given in marriage, the family as a whole aids in the process of guidance so that the implications of a blind decision can be exposed and weighed out. Its impact on the whole family could be catastrophic, and therefore the families participate to a degree.

The same is true in all community-centric cultures, and it goes far beyond a man and a woman being well suited to each other. The crops are harvested together, and the hunting and preparation for the changing seasons are done together. Whether it's agricultural or industrial, everyone has found a place and the interconnectedness makes the whole stronger than the sum of its individual parts.

Both the Old and New Testaments were inspired within a culture of community. The early church worshiped and lived communally. The Bible provides a detailed snapshot of what the church looked like at the beginning:

> They devoted themselves to the apostles' teaching and to fellowship, to the breaking of bread and to prayer. Everyone was filled with awe at the many wonders and signs performed by the apostles. All the believers were together and had everything in common. They sold property and possessions to give to anyone who had need. Every day they continued to meet together in the temple courts. They broke bread in their homes and ate together with glad and sincere hearts, praising God and enjoying the favor of all the people. And the Lord added to their number daily those who were being saved. (Acts 2:42 – 47)

Don't worry: I'm not going to tell you to sell all your things, send the proceeds to my PO box, and move into a hotel for Christians. But I do want to point out how the Western culture we've been born into celebrates our individuality to the point that self-absorption has practically become the norm. We unwittingly drag all this cultural baggage into our faith, and somehow we equate our personal comfort and desires with closeness to God. If we're happy and in plenty, he is near, we reason. If we're facing hardship and challenge, we believe God has moved away. Often the opposite is true.

Too often we experience faith in a solitary way. We rarely think of it in terms of "us" and "our," and frequently see it as "me" and "my." Although our Western culture has many beautiful aspects to it, and the society we live in is what we know and understand, we can't mistake its individualistic values for biblical values. Community is irreplaceable in the Christian life, and we are all connected. The apostle Paul describes it this way:

> Just as a body, though one, has many parts, but all its many parts form one body, so it is with Christ. For we were all baptized by one Spirit so as to form one body — whether Jews or Gentiles, slave or free — and we were all given the one Spirit to drink. (1 Corinthians 12:12 – 13)

The rest of 1 Corinthians 12 beautifully illustrates how one part of the body cannot say to another that it's not needed, and when one part is hurting, the whole body suffers.

I know a retired doctor named Wooly who deeply loves Jesus. In conversation with him a few years ago he illuminated my understanding of how our bodies are brilliant examples of the body of Christ. He described how the head is the control center of the body. It makes millions of decisions subconsciously per second and directs impulses throughout the nervous system at about seven hundred miles an hour. When something in the body blocks these instructions from getting through, sickness and disease begin to develop.

"The body has enormous built-in power to recreate and regenerate itself," Dr. Wooly explained. "It can fight interlopers like viruses and infections that might otherwise cause harm or death. The Bible tells us we are the body of Christ and Christ is the head of the church. Jesus is like the brain, and sin is the inhibitor that keeps the instructions from getting through to the body's organs."

If we're all interconnected as the body of Christ, it's not possible to be free-standing, isolated entities. It's not possible to survive without each other. The bad news is that living in community requires sacrifice. The good news is that we can survive and thrive in community. The great news is that we have permission to be ourselves. We're uniquely placed. Our role is irreplaceable and our value immeasurable. A good many of the troubles that arise in community seem to come from our brokenness and insecurity, and so much of this happens because we ultimately think we're on our own and that we can survive that way. We can't.

When the body works together fighting against that which would kill it, whether from within or without, there is enormous power to heal, restore, and renew what was sick and dying. When the body begins to attack itself, it dies.

We find a better sense of our own story as we share our life with one another. In their stories we find common ground. We can relate to their victories and their struggles, and we can witness God's hand in their lives — at times before even they themselves do—and that can be a big part of the individual journey.

—Jim, Massachusetts

Obsession, Control, and the Predator

One of the oddest things I've observed among believers is the massive amount of energy we can spend trying to be in control of nearly every eventuality and circumstance of life. This manifests itself in all sorts of ugly ways that we're all probably familiar with, but the greatest horror is that in our scuffles, conflict, and retaliation, we forget that we actually have a mortal enemy who wants us all dead. A lot of times the idea of spiritual opposition to our very existence isn't even a category we pay attention to, but it's one that we ignore at our own peril.

Have you ever watched one of those nature shows on television where a pack of lions or wolves is hunting for dinner? Normally the predator will observe from a distance and carefully stalk an unsuspecting herd of gazelles or zebras, quietly waiting for just the right moment to charge. Once spooked, the herd begins to move. They protect their young as best as they can, but as they pick up speed, they fragment ever so slightly. This is the moment the predators are looking for. When an elderly animal or a young one can't keep up or gets separated from its community, it becomes an easy kill. The same principles apply to the Christian life.

In his first letter, the apostle Peter says, "Be alert and of sober mind. Your enemy the devil prowls around like a roaring lion looking for someone to devour. Resist him, standing firm in the faith, because you know that the family of believers throughout the world is undergoing the same kind of sufferings" (1 Peter 5:8–9).

I was in South Africa a couple of months ago and had the privilege of visiting Kruger National Park for a few days. The park is as large as the country of Israel, and it's about as wild a place as it gets. Near the Orpen Dam we came upon a pride of nine lions devouring a giraffe. This is not a pretty sight, especially for the giraffe. This ripping of hide, tearing of raw meat from bone, cracking, grunting, and growling process of completely consuming its prey is what the apostle Peter warns is our enemy's intentions for us. Peter begs us to be alert and to be of sober mind regarding this fact.

If we choose to avoid community and do not engage in fellowship with each other, we become easy targets. If we spend our time squabbling, we're definitely not alert and sober of mind toward the enemy of our lives; instead, we're in danger of becoming separated from the rest and of being devoured. We can't survive long outside of community. We're not made for it.

Once we understand with clarity that community is vital to our spiritual survival, we can begin to celebrate the beauty of how God has woven us together as one body and how important we are to each other's survival. Together we can participate in the abundant life Scripture describes; apart from each other we cannot.

If we are the body of Christ as the Bible declares and we cannot separate ourselves from one another and survive, then the Bible is one of the most indispensable resources God has provided to give balance on the high seas of life in community. The Bible gives us our orientation to God and the baseline for processing the drama each day brings. It challenges our motivations and gives us the deep wisdom it takes to function as the body of Christ.

Who We Are Together

Throughout this book I hope I've been making a compelling case for the necessity of having Scripture in our lives each day. But as important and irreplaceable as it is as individuals, it is even more important to the life of the body of Christ, the life of a community.

Not only is it far more risky to try to live a private life of faith; it's also impossible, and misunderstanding this is perilous to our future. The Bible is an active participant in what God has been and continues to do in the world, and God invites us to participate in that work. The writer of Hebrews says, "The word of God is alive and active. Sharper than any double-edged sword, it penetrates even to dividing soul and spirit, joints and marrow; it judges the thoughts and attitudes of the heart" (Hebrews 4:12). This is not a weak pastime or optional hobby we should consider. Its words will show us who we are apart and who we could be together.

I have seen firsthand what the Bible can do when it is the basis for community. I am convinced that our online community that is passionately committed to daily interaction with Scripture can be replicated in localized communities everywhere just as it was with ancient Israel when they were freed from Egyptian bondage. When our passion for God and the way he reveals himself so beautifully in his Word becomes the central basis for our fellowship with one another, we continually stay oriented to the things that actually matter, and we remember who we are — the body of Christ.

When Christ came to rescue the world from the bondage of sin and death (Romans 8:2), everything changed; but he left it to us, as in *we* together, to complete the work (Matthew 28:18 – 20). Think about that. When Christ came, he once and for all destroyed the barrier between the Father and men and women caused by sin. This colossal rescue of humanity that had been foretold and foreshadowed for thousands of years was finally complete.

It would seem that all he needed to do was to stick around as the resurrected Savior of the world, and he could have established his kingdom here on earth. It wouldn't have taken that long. After all, when a guy shows up alive after being pummeled beyond recognition and literally nailed to a crossbeam until he was dead, news would travel fast — especially if he started walking the streets again. Had he just gone to the temple, people would have freaked out. It wouldn't have taken long to build momentum and swiftly establish his throne on earth, seeing that he was who he said he was and his resurrection was more than proof. But instead of doing this, Jesus bestowed his authority on us and commissioned us to tell the good news while he went to prepare a place for us (John 14:1 – 3).

That's a lot of trust, but we've been given a lot of authority. Jesus said, "Very truly I tell you, everyone who believes in me will do the works I have been doing, and they will do even greater things than these, because I am going to the Father" (John 14:12). Christ is living in and through us (John 14:20; 17:23; Galatians 2:20; Colossians 1:27), and we, in community, are the hands and feet of Jesus in this world. As such we are commissioned and commanded to do the work of heaven on earth. Together, we have the incredible privilege of being participants in his kingdom coming and his will being done on earth as it is in heaven. I've seen the positive effects of community and the way it is aggressively opposed. It has convinced me of its divine power and authority. This is how God has chosen to get his work in this world done.

I am a college student graduating in a week. Yikes. It is almost time to begin packing up all of my stuff once again to move across the country. I am twenty-two and I have already lived in five states (soon to be six). Needless to say, I am used to moving. However, the one thing I have noticed between this impending move and the previous ones is that this time, part of the community I participate in is coming with me. It feels like the entire Daily Audio Bible community will be packing up as well to join me rather than my leaving them behind. This has been a great source of comfort in my life, and I am thankful to feel the love and support offered from God through others to make this move feel less lonely.

I started listening to the Daily Audio Bible because I thought listening with others would help me to be more accountable, which it has, but I never dreamed of how much it would change my outlook on life. Rather than being terrified about having to find a whole new support system, I am now excited to move, knowing that there is still a community with me. Plus, my relationship with God is stronger than it has ever been, so now I have more trust, knowing that by following him, I will end up right where I need to be.

—Rachel, Iowa

Looking beyond the Wounds

Reading the Bible in community at dailyaudiobible.com has been one of the greatest joys and most profoundly impacting things in my life. It is one of the only places I've seen where geography does not prohibit a sense of belonging. On January 1 of each year I begin to read the Bible, starting in Genesis, Matthew, Psalms, and Proverbs (see the reading plans in the back of the book). We work our way through the Old and New Testaments one day at a time until on December 31, we complete the entire journey. It's a seven-day-a-week emersion in God's Word, and because it's happening fresh each and every day, it's dynamic to what is going on in the world and inside the Daily Audio Bible community.

Every year new themes emerge as we progress through these readings together. The website is fully integrated into the community experience so that discussions are taking place around the clock in the forums. There are many chat rooms, and it's always possible to find someone else to talk to. In July 2009 we began to pray "around the world, around the clock," so there's always a place to pray and worship God among other believers by going into the WindFarm Prayer Room on the website.

Over the years it has become abundantly clear that the Bible has a voice and can speak the counsel of God, and this is best lived out in community with each other. Knowing that you can reach out and someone will reach back with no judgment, no stereotype, and no assumptions about who you are has made the Daily Audio Bible a Christ-centered community oriented around the Bible as a place of healing. At the Daily Audio Bible, no matter where you may physically be on this planet, you don't ever have to be alone again.

Living in community with Christ as the head giving instructions to the body through his Holy Spirit is what we were created for. This is what life is supposed to look like. The radical change in the landscape of the world that we long for, both as individuals and collectively, can be achieved no other way.

In spite of all the great stories of encouragement and unity I experience in the Daily Audio Bible community, I know how difficult living as the body of Christ can be. Virtually every faith community includes people who have been wounded by other Christians. They've not given up on God, but they have definitely given up on his people. This is sad. There are forces at play here that are dark and sinister. If we can be divided, we can be conquered; but probably an even more crucial truth is that if we remain divided, we cannot complete the work we are commissioned to do.

I lived an isolated life for many years. Most of my isolation was a reaction to emotional wounds that convinced me it was safer to depend on myself than to trust anyone else. When I was eight years old, I often sang in church. On one occasion, I was accompanied by my father on the piano, but I forgot the words to the song. The audience laughed vigorously as if I were putting on a comedy routine. In all fairness, they were laughing at how cute the scene was, but that's not what it felt like for me. I sank into the stool I was standing on and then walked out of the auditorium with my head hung low, not daring a peek at anyone. No matter how many pats on the back and words of encouragement I got, I felt humiliated. In that moment, I got the message that I was all alone. I bought it, and even at that young age I determined I would never be put in that position again. I would never climb onto a stage and say or sing another word.

Does that seem like an overreaction? As silly as some of our stories might seem, the misguided messages we buy into — whether in childhood or just this past week — can lead us into the kind of separation and isolation that results in being taken out and devoured. I could tell many personal stories of what life looks like isolated and out of community, but I'm guessing we are all familiar with how easy it is for us to get our faith rocked when we stand alone. Sadly, our faith can get rocked when we're in community as well. It's risky. So what are we to do? Love one another.

Commanded To Love

Jesus said, "A new command I give you: Love one another. As I have loved you, so you must love one another. By this everyone will know that you are my disciples, if you love one another" (John 13:34–35). If our lives aren't characterized by love, then we honestly need to ask ourselves why. Jesus is telling us that love is the indicator that we are his disciples. But more than that, he is telling us that we *must* love one another. This is not merely a new suggestion he gave us; it is a command. We cannot ignore it if we are to become authentic disciples of Jesus.

There is a reason for this: love never fails. "And now these three remain," the Bible says, "faith, hope and love. But the greatest of these is love" (1 Corinthians 13:13). Imagine the power wielded by combining faith, hope, and love. It won't look like the latest high-intensity, special-effects movie to come out of Hollywood; but if you apply faith, hope, and love to a soul, from that point on, every experience is transformed. A person cannot remain unaffected. Nothing evil can stand for long in the presence of faith, hope, and love; it will burn away like so much chaff. But the greatest of these is love.

The dictionary defines love as a deep, tender, ineffable feeling of affection and solicitude toward a person, such as that arising from kinship or a sense of underlying oneness. This is the textbook definition of the most powerful force known to humankind—a force that drives even God himself. It sounds remarkably like what the apostle Paul describes when he tells us who we are as the body of Christ.

Paul's famous description of love in 1 Corinthians 13 describes the profound mystery and power of love. We can speak with a gilded tongue, but without love it's of no use. Create what you will but without love, it's less than garbage. We can use the authority of heaven and prophetically know the future and even have the power to demand the snow-capped Rocky Mountains to move out of our path; even if they do, without love the commanding display is worthless. If we give all we have to care for the poor and brokenhearted and but do not do it in love, it simply has no value. It's nothing.

Basically we're being commanded to love one another; if we don't, nothing will work and nothing will matter. The Bible couldn't be clearer on this. This is the posture of community, of marriage, of life. This is what our lives are supposed to look like. What would happen to the world if we actually believed this? What would happen to the body of Christ if we believed it?

The apostle Paul concludes his description of love by saying, "We don't yet see things clearly. We're squinting in a fog, peering through a mist" (1 Corinthians 13:12 MSG). Isn't that how things feel a lot of the time? When we live in a fog, we can't see what or who is around us. We have to slow down and be cautious. If we can be kept in this isolated fog, we are nearly powerless. If we can be kept distracted and unaware of who our enemy actually is, we can be utterly useless. But the Bible promises us clarity. It promises us that the day is coming when we will see God face-to-face. What would it look like if we finally realized that we are woven together as one body? When one hurts, we all hurt. What if we approached community surrendered to the authority of

Scripture and obeyed the command to approach one another always with love?

The Amazon River originates on the side of a cliff called Nevado Mismi in the Andes Mountains of Peru. From this trickle tributaries from far and wide begin to join it in its pursuit of the sea. Near Menous, Brazil, the Rio Negro flowing from Columbia and the Amazon Basin joins the Solimoes from Peru and Brazil. These two major tributaries are so different in their composition that they flow together, and yet do not mix for many miles. This is called Encontro das Águas, the meeting of the waters. As the two become one, they grow significantly more powerful.

By the time the Amazon drains into the Atlantic Ocean, it has so much force it pushes fresh water over two hundred miles into the sea. Salt-free drinking water can be taken out of the ocean completely out of view of land. Large sea vessels come into the drainage to clean salt-water barnacles from their hulls because they cannot live in fresh water. This is the power of community moving in the same direction with one pursuit in mind. This is a picture of who we are and what we're a part of.

CHAPTER 6

LECTIO DIVINA: DIVINE READING

As the deer pants for streams of water,
so my soul pants for you, my God.

   —The Sons of Korah

My sheep listen to my voice;
I know them, and they follow me.

   —Jesus

everal summers ago my friend Brad and I went in search of Bigfoot. This wasn't the original plan, but we got ambitious in our travels between meetings in Idaho and Oregon and decided to drive the Olympic Peninsula as a slight detour. If there is a Bigfoot, it certainly must live in the northwest corner of the continental United States or somewhere similar. Fatigue mixed with wonder was the elixir that got us spinning our own yarns as we wandered along little trails and forest roads. Any creak of a tree or flight of a bird caused a jolt of adrenaline, and we did our best to bring the myth to life for our own childish amusement.

I was certain that Sasquatch would prefer Brad because he's taller and, I believe, more appealing to a hairy beast than me, but Brad was convinced that I would actually be the more tasty morsel or love interest. In the end, the only Bigfoot we found was carved into a tree outside a little outfitter store in the rainforest district of the peninsula. It was everything we'd imagined, although the gender issue was never solved with any certainty.

Inside the little store I had an experience that felt as if the Holy Spirit had taken a moment to draw so close as to whisper softly in my ear. He spoke through the words on a T-shirt:

The journey is the destination.

That single sentence unlocked something so deep inside me that I've never forgotten it. Life and love aren't tasks to be completed. The purpose of each day isn't merely to make it to the next one. Life isn't a race to the end but rather a gift given moment by moment. The destination has no context without the journey. Five words on a T-shirt spoke profound truth to me, not only about my relationship with God but also about why I love beauty and engage so deeply with nature. It's all about loving the journey — experiencing every moment as one filled with God's presence.

Sadly, we are too often a destination-obsessed people. We are so motivated by accomplishment that it's almost impossible for us to have a context for life outside of what we get done. We're task-oriented and productivity-driven. I'm not setting up to take a swing at this because I certainly do believe things need to get done. Responsibility isn't the enemy. But perhaps there is something ugly behind the veneer of efficiency. Perhaps we buy a little too much into what we can do and then delude ourselves into thinking a full life is one that has no room. We know this can't be true, but we don't seem too willing to do anything about it.

The proof is in the way we live crisis to crisis. But are we really living if day after day all we do is get out of bed, coffee up, and attack the day? Are stress levels an indicator of our happiness? Where does God fit into this scheme? Are prayers for strength to get everything done sufficient communication for an intimate relationship? If disruption challenges our agenda, do we go ballistic and redouble our efforts to meet our quotas, whether self-imposed or not? What if the disruption comes from God?

If we want to experience the abundant life God offers, we have to release our controlling, productivity-oriented approach to faith and engaging Scripture. It's only when we surrender ourselves to the journey — wherever it takes us — that we begin to feel the winds of the Spirit blowing freely through our souls.

Wild Goose Chase

In the sixth century, Saint Columba left his native Ireland and sailed into exile in a small boat called a coracle. Tradition has it that he unfurled the sails of his tiny vessel and let the wind itself set his course. Landing along the Scottish coast, he moved northward until he settled on the island of Iona. He was chasing *gé fhiáin*, the Wild Goose, an ancient Celtic symbol of the Holy Spirit. I love this image because following after the Holy Spirit is often counterintuitive. Often we are on a path of obedience that feels counterproductive only to find that we have come to a place in our hearts that needs deep healing or have arrived at an unexpected place of joy. The Spirit leads where we need to go, and that is not always on a path toward our to-do list. Many times we will find ourselves weaving and interlocking like the knotting on an Irish cross.

For Scripture to have the impact we long for and to bring us the life it promises, we have to be willing to follow wherever it leads us. This is going to wreak some havoc on our best-laid plans — especially for those of us who gauge our value with checklists and efficiency quotas. But it is also the only way to discover genuine life.

Let's be honest: we will never find the life we want if we continue on our present course. Instead, we are invited to take a different course, a wild goose chase that may not always seem efficient but will lead to the life we've been killing ourselves with an overburdened to-do list to get. While we give chase, we discover that life is not something we accomplish. It's something we live. This relationship with the Lord isn't about arriving somewhere or achieving something. It's about being somewhere, simply being in the presence of God for the pure joy of it.

We don't merely read the Bible; we live it. That's how we experience life with God. Life on earth is not a waiting game. We were not created simply to go through the motions trying to be good people on our way through to the next round in heaven. Our relationship with God has already begun and eternity is now. Certainly, we will go on, but we need to embrace the fact that we are already in eternity and enjoy every breath as a gift, and to breathe it back as an act of worship. The journey, the twists and turns, the weaving and interlocking, are the destination.

Creating Sacred Space

The Holy Spirit has wild goose access to our lives when we give the Bible sufficient room to speak to us. By room, I mean space in our lives. Jesus is the perfect example of what it means to make space in our lives for God:

- "Very early in the morning, while it was still dark, Jesus got up, left the house and went off to a solitary place, where he prayed" (Mark 1:35).

- "But Jesus often withdrew to lonely places and prayed" (Luke 5:16).

- "When Jesus heard what had happened, he withdrew by boat privately to a solitary place" (Matthew 14:13).

- "Then, because so many people were coming and going that they did not even have a chance to eat, he said to them, 'Come with me by yourselves to a quiet place and get some rest.' So they went away by themselves in a boat to a solitary place" (Mark 6:31 – 32).

Jesus regularly and habitually withdrew to pray and be restored, yet the Bible gives no indication that his ministry (his productivity) suffered as a result. If anything, he was able to accomplish more because he took the time to orient himself to his Father and to renew his body and mind. There are no instances in the Gospels in which Jesus has a nervous breakdown. There are also no depictions of Jesus staring at the twelve disciples blankly wondering what they should do next. His commitment to making space in his life to listen to God was a vital component of his life and ministry.

Trying to keep up with the speed of the world we live in and dealing with the endless distractions and obligations pressing in on every side of our lives threaten the very core of who we are as spiritual beings created in the image of God. In the midst of this kind of life, what would happen if we sat still, even just for five minutes? No texting, no phone calls, no email, no television, no radio, and no Internet. What would five minutes of distraction-free silence be like? What about ten? Fifteen? At what point would we be ready to crawl out of our skin?

Our discomfort with silence, with stillness, reveals how addicted we are to motion. It shapes and defines us. We don't want to be alone without the comfort of something to do, a distraction within arm's reach. Yet, if we are unwilling to withdraw to a solitary place — to make sacred space in our lives for God — we will never be quiet enough to hear the whispers of guidance we need to simply survive, much less experience life to the full.

But let's assume we are willing to set aside the time, then what? How do we give Scripture a spacious place to work in our lives? The answer lies in the ancient Christian practice of *lectio divina*.

Divine Reading

In the early church of the 200s, some Christians chose to withdraw and seek God in the desert as a way of life. They lived an austere and simple existence, focusing their energies on spiritual pursuits rather than material gain or physical comfort. It was in the desert that the ancient practice of *lectio divina* (LEK-tsea-oh di-VEEN-ah) began. *Lectio divina*, Latin for "divine reading," became a foundational practice in the monastic life for many church fathers, including Saint Augustine and Saint Benedict; and it eventually became a common practice among ordinary Christians as well.

Lectio divina is an unhurried, contemplative reading of a portion of Scripture. It provides a framework that allows for deep immersion in God's Word and prayerful consideration of how the Holy Spirit wants to speak to us through it. This is how we make space in our lives to be still and know that he is God (Psalm 46:10).

Saint Benedict encouraged believers to "listen with the ears of our hearts," which is how we hear the voice of God in our lives and how the Scriptures become the Word of God in a real and vibrant way to our spirits.

Lectio divina begins when we withdraw as Jesus did to a quiet or still place. If you've ever been to the desert, you'll have a vivid image of this kind of quiet. The desert is utterly silent and still, which, quite honestly, can be unnerving. The silence actually seems to have a personality of its own, and we're just not used to being that motionless. Before long, the shy sounds of tranquility begin to emerge — the insects, the breeze, even our own heartbeat. This is stillness.

Whether or not we have the ability to escape to the desert isn't the point. We need to quiet regularly the noise of life by arranging for uninterrupted time with God—time in which we have no agenda, no checklist, and no anticipated outcome. When we set aside unhurried time to listen, we give God access to the deepest part of our hearts. We quiet ourselves enough to hear his whispers, the tender truths that heal, restore, and guide.

The book of 1 Kings tells the story of how the prophet Elijah encounters God in the quiet—even though he has to go through a lot of drama to get there. In one of the epic stories in the Bible, Elijah makes a wager with the priests of Baal. They erect an altar to the god Baal, and Elijah repairs the altar of the Lord. The stage is set for the showdown. Everyone agrees that the altar struck by fire from heaven will determine whose god is the true God.

The priests of Baal go first. All through the morning they cry out to Baal to answer them. Noon comes and Elijah arrogantly taunts them. They cry out all the louder, cutting themselves and amping up the frenzy. This goes on until it's time for the evening sacrifice. Elijah prepares the sacrifice to the Lord and even asks for water to be poured all over the altar and the sacrifice. Then Elijah prays, the fire comes, and the people experience a dramatic demonstration of God's power. The priests of Baal are forcibly removed from life, and there's no doubt about whose God wins. But Elijah's euphoria is short-lived. He immediately panics when he gets word that Queen Jezebel is out to kill him because of what has just happened. Elijah runs off into the desert to hide. God meets him in a cave on Mount Horeb.

"What are you doing here?" God asks.

Elijah pours out his sob story—that he is the only one left in the world who is true to God. The same God who had just rained down fire and obliterated an altar in front of thousands of people then tenderly offers Elijah a personal gift. God invites Elijah to go out and stand on the mountain because he is going to pass by.

A great wind tears at the mountain and shatters rocks in a terrifying display of force, but God is not in it. The earth shakes from a mighty earthquake, but God is not in the earthquake. Then a fire rages around Elijah, but God is not present in the fire. Finally, there comes a gentle whisper. Elijah pulls his cloak over his head and steps out to meet God. God comes to him not in noise and force but in quiet and stillness. That's when God tells Elijah what he needs to hear.

This kind of quiet space for listening is what we are seeking when we practice *lectio divina*. We want to hear the gentle whisper that is more powerful than the pull of any distraction, addiction, or obligation. We surrender our desires, habits, stresses, pleasures, or pains and come empty-handed before God, having no agenda other than to allow him access to our hearts and lives.

Four Steps

The practice of *lectio divina* includes four steps:

> *Lectio* (LEK-tsea-oh), read
>
> *Meditatio* (med-i-TA-shee-oh), meditate
>
> *Oratio* (or-A-shee-oh), speak or pray
>
> *Contemplatio* (con-tem-PLA-shee-oh), contemplate or rest

Lectio (Read)

Lectio, the first step, is a slow reading of a brief passage of Scripture while listening for God to speak through it. It may be a passage we feel led to in the moment or one we've selected in advance. Either way, we read it with a listening heart. We invite God to speak to us through it. As we slowly read repeatedly, we look for any word or phrase that draws our attention. When we identify this word or phrase, we then begin to meditate upon it. (Please see sidebar for suggested passages to get you started.)

Psalm 23:	The Lord is my shepherd
Psalm 27:	One thing I ask and desire
Psalm 42:	My soul longs for God
Psalm 46:	Be still and know that I am God
Psalm 91:	Shelter
Isaiah 30:15 – 21:	Quietness and trust
Matthew 11:25 – 30:	Come to Jesus
Luke 1:26 – 38:	The immaculate conception
Luke 5:1 – 11:	To actually be a disciple of Jesus
John 3:1 – 8:	The Spirit gives new life
John 4:4 – 26:	Living water
John 10:4 – 15:	Listening to Jesus, the good shepherd

Meditatio (Meditate)

Meditatio is mediation, a time of quiet reflection in God's presence.[6] The early Christians used the analogy of an animal quietly chewing its cud to describe this kind of meditating on the Scriptures. It's important to keep in mind that the purpose of this step is not to force ourselves into a mystical experience or even a deep insight. Our goal is to focus our affection and attention on God. Where he leads, we will follow.

We quietly read the words he's led us to in Scripture and slowly chew them. We interact with them, invite them to shed light on our thoughts and experiences, and permit God to connect these truths to our lives. Perhaps our attention is drawn to wounds we avoid, blessings we've experienced, dormant dreams we've given up on, or relationships we need to mend. We simply give God permission to bring the truth of Scripture into the most intimate places in our lives without reservation and in full trust.

Quietly, as we focus on the word or phrase, we encourage our thoughts and deepest desires to interact with God's Word. Through this process we allow it to become his personal Word to us, speaking directly to our issues, decisions, hopes, and dreams — and his will for us in all of it. The psalmist said, "I have hidden your word in my heart that I might not sin against you" (Psalm 119:11). This is a clear representation of what we are doing as we meditate and interact with Scripture. After listening to God, the next step is to respond to what we've heard.

Oratio (Pray)

The third step in *lectio divina* is *oratio* or prayer. We respond to what God has spoken to us through Scripture.

We often think of prayer as primarily talking *to* God, but what Scripture invites us to is conversational intimacy *with* God. In following the steps of *lectio divina*, we still ourselves and listen before we utter a single request or appeal. We've allowed God to initiate the conversation, and what a difference it makes as we enter into this step of *oratio*. We are in the presence of God. We feel his loving embrace around us even though what he may be speaking is discipline.

We aren't coming to God with demands and petitions;

rather, we're consecrating ourselves and asking that he take his Word into the deepest and most intimate places in our lives. We're agreeing with what he's spoken and receiving the truth into ourselves while offering him our broken lives and inviting his Word to change us irreversibly. We're inviting Christ into the places he's exposed or the moments he's taken us back to so that he might heal us and set us free (Luke 4:18).

In *oratio*, we offer God our worship and agree with his Word and his will. We rejoice in his presence and enjoy a time of authentic conversation that is unhurried and not self-absorbed, for we are seeing things from God's perspective and have aligned our hearts with his. Then we are prepared to rest in God's love and care.

Contemplatio (Contemplate)

In the final step of *lectio divina*, we enter into *contemplatio* or contemplation, a time of rest. Here we entrust ourselves to God as we reflect on what he has spoken. We listen for any other words he may want to speak. We remain as still and close as friends or lovers who do not have the frantic need to fill the space with words. God has spoken through his Word, we have allowed him access to the places in our lives he wants to go, and we have agreed with his will and offered ourselves in worship. In *contemplatio* we come to a place of reverence and silence once again as we are released to fulfill God's purposes for us that day.

Growing in Love

Jesus gave us two great commandments: to love the Lord our God with all our heart, soul, and mind, and to love our neighbor as ourselves (Matthew 22:37 – 39). He also commissioned us to "go and make disciples of all nations, baptizing them in the name of the Father and of the Son and of the Holy Spirit, and teaching them to obey everything I have commanded you" (Matthew 28:19 – 20a). Jesus bestowed his authority on us to do these things (Matthew 28:18; Mark 16:17 – 18), promised always to be with us (Matthew 28:20b), and sent the Holy Spirit to guide and counsel us in the process (John 14:26). In other words, he equipped us to live and love as he did.

No matter what other obligations in life we may have and no matter what else we accomplish, the two great commandments and Great Commission are central to the life of every believer. They form the trunk from which springs the branches of life. In practicing regular times of *lectio divina*, we not only allow the Holy Spirit to remind us of who we are and what our mission is; we also grow in intimacy with God. As this intimacy deepens, we become more like Christ.

CHAPTER 7

THE SPOKEN WORD, THE LIVING VOICE

Handle them carefully,
for words have more power than atom bombs.
— Pearl Strachan

Words can be short and easy to speak,
but their echoes are truly endless.
— Mother Teresa

Those who have ears to hear, let them hear.
— Jesus

At age sixteen I had a life-changing experience during a worship service at a Hillsong Conference. It was my first experience of feeling close to God! With my eyes closed and hands reaching up there was nothing that could convince me God wasn't right there. Following that encounter, I developed an addiction to reading the Bible. I had to have it! I read it on the bus to school, I read it before school, during lunch times, on the bus home, and again at home. It was like my best friend, and reading it ushered in my awareness of the Holy Spirit. I often smiled or just cried at the perfect way God worked.

As time passed, my love for the Bible diminished as other things took my focus. When I did pick up the Bible, I often felt it didn't make sense or that I'd already read it anyway. I really wanted my love for the Bible back, but I didn't know what to do.

Last September I listened to the Bible being read aloud for the first time. I began participating in the reading of the Scriptures out loud and I'm addicted again! I love God's Word! I love the sense of community and family I feel from processing the Scriptures together with other believers.

— Marc, Australia

I was sitting in a South African patio cafe one morning with my missionary friend Mike. We were an hour into the five-hour trek back to Johannesburg in order to catch my return flight to America, and we'd randomly selected this little cafe for breakfast because its sign touted ruins of an ancient civilization.

We enjoyed an English breakfast of eggs, tomato, sausage, and beans while flipping through two books the owner had written about the ruins that covered hundreds of square miles of real estate on this part of the continent. Shortly after, the writer himself welcomed us to his little bistro, and we began to ask obvious questions like, "Where might we see such ruins?" He replied with an expansive hand gesture to the whole of the area.

"They are all around you," he said. "You are in the middle of the largest city complex the world has ever known." He went on to tell us that the ruins covered more than a thousand kilometers and that research had shown the current ruins were built on much older civilizations that were destroyed in a great flood that he believed to be the flood of Noah.

"What would support such a vast civilization in such a primitive time?" I asked. "Why did people settle here?"

"Gold," he answered as a twinkle appeared in his eye. "This is where I believe the gold of Ophir came from."

He then spoke of Solomon and his alliance with the Queen of Sheba, who is traditionally believed to be African. He quoted from Genesis 2:11 – 12, which names four great rivers: "The name of the first is the Pishon; it winds through the entire land of Havilah, where there is gold. (The gold of that land is good; aromatic resin and onyx are also there.)"

"We are, I believe, in ancient Havilah," he said. He paused

and then added, "Why would the Bible talk about how good the gold was at the beginning of history if it weren't important? What did that have to do with anything?"

We acknowledged that we had no idea, and we began to wonder if we'd met a loopy new age guru or a bona fide scientist who could perhaps fill in some missing chunks of ancient history.

The conversation turned to the fact that I had worked in the Christian music industry. At one point in the writer's life, he had come to America to record in Nashville; he planned to return when he toured the States to promote a third book about the ruins that he was currently in the process of writing.

Then he said it.

"It's very interesting, this talk of music and its power to speak to people. How do you think these ancient civilizations did such things like dredging mines, erecting buildings, and even constructing the massive Egyptian pyramids with such primitive knowledge?"

Again we shrugged our shoulders in ignorance.

"They had technology we've forgotten," he said. "They knew the power of sound. They knew that sound is energy and they harnessed it to move things. We can't figure out how they did it, even though we know the principles of it."

I thought the conversation was going to turn to cosmic vibrations and other metaphysically laced ideas, but he again turned to Scripture.

"In the beginning was the *Word*," he said, quoting from the gospel of John. Then back to the book of Genesis, "And God *said*, 'Let there be light.' And God *said*, 'Let there be an expanse between the waters.' And God *said*, 'Let the water under the sky be gathered together in one place and let dry ground appear.' The power is in the living voice. The power is in the sound."

"Wow," I said.

In that moment something clicked. I told Mike as we drove away that this felt important somehow and I thought a lot about this encounter during the following weeks.

The Spoken Word Is Powerful

Words spoken aloud are some of the most common but also most intriguing things in human experience. They form in our hearts and develop like film in the darkroom of our minds. We transfer them to our tongues, squeeze them by our cheeks, and slide them across our lips. They construct a living narrative and in the process set the tone and pace of life. They bring tears, smiles, rage, desire, compassion, and every other human emotion that we feel. They can draw us together in perfect intimacy or force us apart with a single sentence. The same sentence spoken in a different tone of voice can yield a completely different emotional response. The vast majority of our emotional reactions are triggered by spoken words.

I've tried in the past to read the Bible from cover to cover. I always gave up in frustration, usually reaching a passage in the OT that either outraged me (the constant violence was and is very hard for me to deal with) or bored me (the long, long lists of begats, etc.). I would usually skip ahead to the NT, where I could be consoled by Christ's sensible answers and his kindness and forgiveness and tolerance. More often than not, I used the drop-the-finger approach, expecting that God would lead me to the passage I needed for that day. Sometimes it worked but after several years it was a book that sadly gathered dust on the shelf!

Then I started listening to the Bible read aloud in a community experience. I was almost instantly hooked. I found that this method was so much more enlightening! I began to think that this was the best way to read the Bible.

I also found that hearing the Bible gives it an authority that is different than silent reading. And something I had rarely done alone was to conclude my Scripture reading with prayer. In community, we always conclude with prayer and it is so fulfilling. Previously, I would pray or I would read the Bible but never at the same time. This unified approach has not only kept me interested, but it has kept me inspired and I can feel it filling me with the Spirit.

—Paul, American in England

Words can be whimsical and serendipitous. They can make us smile for joy at the way they're strung together, whether they make sense or not. They can also sear themselves into our memories and leave a tattoo on our souls.

The last word my father ever said to me was, "Okay." This was his response to my telling him that I'd see him the following day. The following day he was gone, and in the ensuing months of working through the loss and grief, I never had any regrets about the things I wished I had thought or written about him. I did regret, however, all the things I never took the time to say out loud.

A Brief History of God's Word — Spoken and Written

There are nearly 7,000 unique languages currently spoken on Planet Earth[7] and almost 40,000 dialects of those languages.[8] Of these unique languages, it is unknown how many have a cohesive system of reading and writing because fewer than 1,000 people speak some of them. Ninety-five percent of the world's languages are spoken by 5 percent of the world's population.[9]

Speaking aloud has always been the primary mode of communication among human beings. People average about 6,000 words per day,[10] and texting and email notwithstanding, that's a lot of sound.

The Bible has been translated into fewer than 2,300 languages; of these translations, many contain only the four Gospels or perhaps the entire New Testament. Some have only one gospel or perhaps only the Psalms.[11] Believers in North America, by contrast, typically have not just one Bible but several. We take it for granted that Bibles are readily available for everyone — but they aren't. In some places in the world, the Bible cannot be translated and handed to a person because their language has no alphabet. The only mode of bringing the gospel is to speak it out loud.

Before it was a bestselling book, the Bible was the spoken Word of God. Much of the Torah (Old Testament) was originally transmitted orally. The ancient Jewish culture into which God chose to reveal himself and his Word was an oral culture. In fact, the earliest evidence of a Hebrew alphabet was discovered at Tel Zayit in Israel, dating to about 1000 BC.[12] This is significantly more recent than the culture itself, which dates to about a thousand years earlier.

To ordinary folks in ancient times, writing was like magic. People were stunned and amazed that these strange etchings on a clay pot or animal skin could produce words, which could be repeated by anyone who could decipher them. It was much like the incredible phenomenon in more recent history of being able to record the human voice and then play it back again. These things that we take for granted today were once marvels. The written word was a mystical thing reserved for those in authority. Priests used it to create religious awe among the worshipers long before literacy was common among ordinary people.

It wasn't until the rise of the Assyrian Empire in 800 BC that a concerted effort was made to promote reading and writing throughout Jewish society. The Assyrians used literacy as a means to further the agenda of the expanding empire,[13] and the conquered Jewish people were likely among the benefactors of this initiative. Archaeological evidence suggests that by the seventh century BC this trend finally reached Jerusalem. The archaeological evidence coincides with the biblical narrative describing the sweeping reforms of King Josiah as he led the Jewish people back to God at the end of the seventh century BC. The spoken Word of God was the preeminent mode of transference for centuries before it was possible for an ordinary person to read it.

The idea of printing the written word by mechanical means originated in China around the time of the early Christian church at the beginning of the third century AD,[14] but it was hundreds of years later before it progressed to the point of wider public availability.

Then, in the mid-fifteenth century AD the famous Gutenberg press changed everything. The dog-eared, hand-written copies of documents being passed around was now over as multiple copies of the same book could be reproduced with relative speed. By the time the Age of Enlightenment came around in the seventeenth century, books were widely available and voraciously read. The Bible had finally transitioned fully to the written Word of God.

This brief history lesson is important because we need to understand the vital role the spoken word has had in shaping the Bible. Knowing how the Bible developed over time and eventually transitioned from oral tradition to the written word also raises some questions. Is it possible that we now consider reading the Bible (silently) more important than experiencing the Bible as a spoken narrative, a living word? If so, what might we be missing?

Hearing the Word

In Jewish synagogues a scroll was, and continues to be, reverently unrolled so the Word of God might be carefully read aloud during worship. In many Christian traditions, the written Word of God is actually carried out among the congregants and read aloud, symbolizing how the Word resides with God's people. Even in contemporary evangelical churches, the Word of God is read aloud at least as part of a sermon.

Here's my point: interacting with Scripture on a daily basis is of vital importance, but that interaction can be expressed in many ways. There is more to it than simply reading a chapter silently with our morning toast and coffee. The apostle Paul declares, "Consequently, faith comes from *hearing* the message, and the message is *heard* through the word about Christ" (Romans 10:17, emphasis added).

There is significant historical precedent for reading the Bible aloud. Scripture itself is full of instances that illustrate the power of what is spoken aloud, whether the words come from the mouth of God or the mouths of human beings. Here are just a few passages that describe that power:

In Genesis 1, God doesn't somehow muse, "Let there be light." God *speaks* the world into existence.

King David prayed, "Set a guard over my mouth, O LORD; keep watch over the door of my lips" (Psalm 141:3).

Many of the Proverbs deal with what comes out of the mouth, but none more eloquently than this: "The tongue has the power of life and death, and those who love it will eat its fruit" (Proverbs 18:21). The power of life and death is hanging there right between our teeth!

The prophet Isaiah uses a staggeringly beautiful metaphor to present God's promise about the power of his Word:

> As the rain and the snow
>   come down from heaven,
> and do not return to it
>   without watering the earth
> and making it bud and flourish,
>   so that it yields seed for the sower
>   and bread for the eater,
> so is my word that goes out from my mouth:
>   It will not return to me empty,
> but will accomplish what I desire
>   and achieve the purpose for which I sent it.
>   (Isaiah 55:10–11)

When Jesus announced his ministry and the reason he had come, he chose to do it while reading the Bible aloud (Luke 4). Jesus entered his home synagogue in Nazareth, unfolded the scroll of the prophet Isaiah, and read aloud from Isaiah 61. When he finished, he rolled the scroll back up and sat down. He sat there, letting the words sink in. All eyes were intently on him before he stated regarding that prophecy: "Today this scripture is fulfilled in your *hearing*" (Luke 4:16–21, emphasis added).

The gospel of John explains beautifully that the Word was in the beginning with God and that without him nothing was made that has been made. The Word became flesh and made his dwelling among us in the person of Jesus (John 1:1–14).

Hebrews 12 describes how the sound of God's voice shakes the earth and the heavens.

James 3 goes into vivid detail of the need for taming the tongue because it is like the rudder of a ship and guides the body.

We could go on and on, exhaustively reviewing what the Bible has to say about the power of spoken words. It tells us to encourage one another with words and to declare things with words. It tells us that our words can be a fountain of life or a death blow. Throughout, it demonstrates a clear precedent for interacting with the Word of God, using our living voices (Proverbs 10:11; 18:21; Romans 10:9; 1 Thessalonians 4:18). So why do we generally choose to interact with the Bible only in silence?

I do not mean to diminish the power of the written word. I have, after all, *written* this book. In no way do I feel that quiet contemplation of the Word of God is a secondary approach to Scripture. But I do feel we are missing out if we limit our interaction with the Bible to silent reading. And I am convinced that the benefits of reading the Bible out loud and hearing it read aloud are more substantial than we realize.

I've read through the Bible before with an individual study plan from our church. We began in Genesis and Matthew, so Old and New Testament readings at the same time, every day. It was really hard for me. I pushed on through it but didn't really enjoy it. Anytime I heard people push to focus on reading Scripture every day, I kind of cringed. I was happy to be able to say that "YES! I read through the Bible in its entirety!" but for some reason the text itself didn't come fully alive to me.

I've had a totally different experience hearing the Bible spoken. I look forward to hearing God's Word; Scripture is coming alive to me. I am amazed at how fast the time goes by and how fast we move through Scripture, but it isn't rushed. Many times I find myself wanting to hear more. That has never happened to me before. I also want to have my Bible nearby so I can mark things that stand out, and re-read parts I'd like to dive into more. Hearing the Bible read aloud is totally my preferred way of being in the Word every day.

—Sheila, Pacific Northwest

I have read the Bible aloud in the company of others every day for over six years. The experience has changed my outlook on just about everything. My perspective on how we are all interconnected has been radically changed. I no longer look at myself as an individual only but as part of the body of Christ and part of the Bible's larger story. I have a completely different view about why I am here and what it really means to become the person God created me to be.

Stewarding this gorgeous planet that God has given us, for

example, is a much higher priority for me than it once was. I have an increasing sense of urgency about transferring faith in the God I love to the next generation. I attribute these changes to the power of God's Word, but I believe firmly that the impact has been greatly magnified by reading it aloud. Speaking it myself and hearing it spoken by others makes God's Word something that has been declared as true rather than something yet to be considered and decided on.

And I know this isn't my experience alone. The thousands upon thousands of emails that have passed through my inbox over these years have confirmed my belief that the Word of God spoken — individually or in community — has remarkable power and authority.

Out Loud and Together

As your view of the Bible begins to transition from seeing it as a sacred object to embracing it as a beloved friend, give it voice. Read it aloud. Listen to it being read. Read it together with others. Speaking the Word orally and receiving it aurally engage your mind and heart in ways silent contemplation may not. Join or create a community that together reads the Bible out loud. The astonishing thing that happens is that our living voices give God's Word a living voice — one we can literally hear.

I have been a Christian for nearly eighteen years and I have found that listening to the Bible has been the best way for me. I have tried to read the Bible on my own but have given up. I do take time to personally reflect on a verse or chapter and I do find that helpful, but I know my life is changing for the better as I read the Bible aloud with others. Something in me is shifting.

—Jane, Lincolnshire, UK

Listening to the Bible being read aloud in community offers us the opportunity to work through its application together. We can talk through questions that would otherwise go unaddressed, and we have the benefit of other people's perspective and wisdom. This also opens up a wonderful means for those who are strong in the faith to mentor those who are new to the faith (1 Thessalonians 5:12; 1 Timothy 5:17; Hebrews 13:17).

I am utterly convinced that giving the Word of God a living voice is giving God a voice. These are his living words, the ones that tell the great story of God among us. As we speak them, we give them power in our lives. Jesus said that it is from the abundance of our hearts that our mouth speaks (see Matthew 12:34). When we speak the living Word of God with our own voices or listen to the Word of God spoken aloud, we open our hearts to the truths contained within the Word of God in a profound way.

The spiritual payoff far outweighs the effort. What was once blurry and cryptic comes into focus; what was once unapproachable and flat becomes accessible and full of life. If we give ear to the words of life, in the listening we will hear the voice of our heavenly Father as he speaks directly to our hearts.

CHAPTER 8

LIVING THE BIBLE IN YOUR FAMILY

No matter what you've done for yourself or for humanity, if you can't look back on having given love and attention to your own family, what have you really accomplished?

— Elbert Hubbard

You don't choose your family. They are God's gift to you, as you are to them.

— Desmond Tutu

My son, if your heart is wise, then my heart will be glad.

— Solomon

My name's Iona. I'm fourteen years old and I live in England. Since I became a Christian a couple of years ago, I've tried to read the whole Bible, but just haven't been able to do it! I sometimes find it difficult to concentrate and so what I've read doesn't always sink in. I prayed for God to help me find a new way to learn in the Bible, and ten minutes later, I came across the Daily Audio Bible! In addition to having a structured way to go through the whole Bible, I can listen to it, which is a lot easier.

My family are not Christians. It can be hard being a Christian girl with non-Christian parents. Don't get me wrong, they're really great people and I know they love me a lot—but the fact that they aren't Christians has had an effect on me. My dad has all sorts of theories as to how the world was made and whether God exists. He says that he is not an atheist, but doesn't believe in God either—he is an agnostic. I think my mom believes in God but she doesn't pray or try to follow Jesus. The fact that she isn't really a proper Christian prevents me from talking to her about normal teenage girl stuff like fights with my friends and boys, as everything I do involves God and she doesn't really understand that. When she was my age she got drunk at late night parties and had a different boyfriend each week!

I don't want to do that and she seems quite surprised about it!

I'm getting to know God better every day and becoming more confident in myself. The Daily Audio Bible has been helpful as I don't often get to go to church or regularly hear people preaching or reading the Bible.

— Iona (a Jesus freak in the making!),
from England

A few evenings ago, my wife was out with some girlfriends, so I was having dinner at a local eatery with three of my kids. Before the food arrived, they decided they wanted to play the "Dis Game." I hadn't heard of this one before but recognized it within a few seconds.

In this "game," one person starts by insulting the other and the insulted person has to respond to the insult with an even greater insult. For example, one child might say, "I never forget a face, but in your case I'll have to make an exception." The offended would then reply, "Yeah, well, everyone has the right to be ugly, but you seem to be abusing the privilege." The initiator would then say, "Keep talking. You might accidentally say something intelligent," to which the offended would laugh and say, "Your mom."

I actually let this go on for a few minutes, recalling the same kind of sparring in my own childhood, but then I couldn't tolerate the cruelty of it. I considered for a moment the way adults play the same game in real life but cloak it in subtlety or sarcasm. Or the sparring battles that husbands and wives can have with the gloves off and every weakness exposed, trying to either get the upper hand in a situation or just to vent terrible amounts of pent-up frustration.

I stopped the Dis Game, but rather than instructing the kids about the bad habits and the terrible hurt this game could cause in our family, I changed the rules. I told them, "All right, now you're going to play the 'Flatter Game.'"

They looked confused. "That's right. The way this works is that you choose your sparring partner and say something kind about them, and they have to give you an even kinder response than you gave. You then get the chance to respond and if you can't outdo them, you lose."

Within ninety seconds my kids were telling each other things like:

"You are very caring."

"You always look out for how everyone feels."

"You have really pretty hair."

"You always make me laugh."

I was quite pleased when my older son told his sister that she had just been "owned" at the Flatter Game by her little brother.

Over the years our memories pile up and place a melancholy smile on our faces, but unfortunately they're often tempered with regret. Most of us at some point try to figure out how to protect our children from some of the lessons we learned the hard way, and for the Christian parent we constantly wonder if we're doing our part in leading them down the right paths.

In All Honesty

You and I have spent a lot of time together now. You've invested a few dollars for this book and several hours into reading it, and I have spent an awful lot of time praying over it and struggling to string all these words together to make this connection. I'd like to think we're friends now. Friends are honest with each other.

I have no doubt of the love you have for your kids. Sure, they can be frustrating and push all your buttons and shred every bit of selfishness you were trying to hold onto. I know what a sacrifice it is and what a priceless gift it is to have them in our lives, and I know of the daunting thoughts that roll in like a dark cloud when we consider their futures and our responsibility in it.

As Christian parents we often fret about our children's spirituality, and it can lead us on a path similar to every other avenue of life. A lot of times we trick ourselves into feeling as if we're making progress by simply staying on the run doing something. There are plenty of resources available in Western civilization to equip parents of any style to make learning the Bible a pure delight for their kids. But I also know that none of it will work. Truthfully, no amount of construction paper and crayons and pictographs and story times or DVD series will work — at least not on their own.

At the risk of sounding overly dramatic, the Bible isn't something to be trifled with. If you're a believer, its pages provide vivid testimony about just how hard it is to live in a fallen world. If anything, it's an honest look at the human struggle forward to God. It's also the story of God's struggle to offer us what our hearts deeply long for, and although he is sovereign, he simply will not build a bridge that forfeits our will. It's a big deal to God that we answer his calling freely, and it will be no different inside our families. Our children will not be coerced into an intimate relationship with Jesus by default. We must show the way by how we live, and we must trust that they will see it. This will not happen if we can't clearly see it ourselves.

Before Jesus laid down his life, he told the disciples that he would be going to prepare a place for us (John 14:1–3). Once the work on the cross was complete and Jesus had returned to life victorious, he commissioned us with his authority to go into the world and make disciples (Matthew 28:18–20).

This starts at home.

I can't even begin to say how happy I am to hear the Bible being read by kids. My two young children and I listen to the Daily Audio Bible for Kids podcast after dinner with ice cream or pudding of some sort. My son is so excited about the Bible because he hears China and her daddy, mommy, and brother Max conversing and praying, he even asks to listen. I particularly remember one episode where Max was being silly and every time he said "Hello" in his funny way, my daughter would laugh and say in a baby way, "Ello"; it was so sweet it almost made me cry.

These are wonderful memories. My children will know the Bible to be fun and interactive. I can see that my son's opinion has changed because the Bible is now a part of his life and he now hears someone not far in age from him reading it and talking with her parent and praying just like we do at home.

My daughter is only a baby but I know she feels involved.

—Sarah Jane, from London, UK

Everything Matters

The lessons and values we learn in our families of origin are etched deeply on our hearts — positively and negatively. This is just as true for your children as it is for you.

Kids pick up on so much more than we think. They are more intuitive than we sometimes give them credit for — and they are watching. As a baseline, until they can reason and rationalize for themselves, they assume that what we say and how we live is "right." And what they learn is not easily unlearned.

The effect we have on our children is far more profound than we ever realize in the moment. It likely won't be until our children are grown and we have the wisdom of clear hindsight — and perhaps the joys of grandchildren — that we understand the profound impact our choices have on our children. This is nothing new. Our choices and the posture of our lives matter greatly both to us and to our kids. The children of Israel learned this lesson in a sobering way, and their children paid a price.

In the book of Exodus, God dramatically frees his people from bondage in Egypt. You are probably familiar with the story. Moses confronts Pharaoh: "Let my people go." Pharaoh refuses to yield to the God of Israel, which results in a series of plagues and great hardship for the Egyptians. The firstborn sons throughout Egypt die in a final showdown, but Israel is spared at the first Passover. At last, the great exodus takes place, and God's people are not only freed from slavery but loot their former captors on the way out without even drawing a sword! Then they experience a supernatural crossing of the Red Sea on dry ground while the pursuing Egyptians are drowned.

The whole story is an amazing display of God's mighty

power. It's hard to imagine how anyone who experienced something like this could ever doubt God or fail in their devotion to him. But it happened. There was a great disconnect between what God's people experienced and how they lived their lives. Shortly after their dramatic deliverance, the children of Israel begin to complain and even to reminisce with longing about their days in slavery. After all that God had done and was continuing to do on their behalf, they nevertheless grumbled against and rejected him. Finally, when God's endless patience had run out, he condemned a whole generation of Israelites to wander in the wilderness for forty years. The generation of promise would not enter the Promised Land. This would be left for the emerging generation.

As familiar as this story is, there is something we often overlook. It is utterly devastating to consider what this experience meant for the children. These little ones had been destined to grow up in a land flowing with milk and honey. They were supposed to be safe on the other side of the Jordan River, enjoying peace and rejoicing in the wonder of their all-powerful, ever-present God. Instead, they grew up wandering aimlessly in the desert, all because their parents chose to worship other gods, to grumble and complain about what they did not have, and ultimately, to abuse God's kindness. They brought judgment on themselves and doomed their children to growing up in a harsh and unforgiving wasteland. It wasn't until they were adults themselves that these little ones entered the Promised Land that should have been their childhood home.

There are parallels between this story and the state of the world today that should tug at our hearts and possibly bring us to our knees. We too find ourselves bowing the knee to false gods. Certainly it's not to an idol that we have created out of spoons and forks, but they are there nonetheless. Perhaps it's money or power; maybe we're starved for megadoses of affirmation because we're still trying to fill the void given to us as children. These things are being transferred to our children in ways that we may not understand. When we grumble and complain about what we do not have and cannot find a place of trusting satisfaction, we are saying to God the same things spoken through the lives of the Israelites in the exodus, and the longer it takes for us to arrive at a place of freedom in Christ, the more we force our children to wander along with us. We must consider what we are doing and what we are leaving undone.

One of the most dramatic instructions in the entire Bible is found in the book of Deuteronomy. Moses is about to die. The children of Israel have known no other leader, and, after forty years, they are once again on the banks of the Jordan preparing to cross over into the Promised Land. Everything they've struggled for and dreamed of is finally at hand, and Moses gives them his final admonition:

> Hear, O Israel: The LORD our God, the LORD is one. Love the LORD your God with all your heart and with all your soul and with all your strength. These commandments that I give you today are to be on your hearts. Impress them on your children. Talk about them when you sit at home and when you walk along the road, when you lie down and when you get up. Tie them as symbols on your hands and bind them on your foreheads. Write them on the doorframes of your houses and on your gates. (Deuteronomy 6:4–9)

Moses tells the Israelites to do whatever they have to so that they will not forget who they are. In order to live under the blessing of the Lord, they must honor and obey him. They must love God and pursue his commandments as a way of life. And they must pass on their faith to the emerging generation, or all will be lost.

What was true for God's people at that time is still true for God's people today. It has not been recalled or revised or updated. This posture of heart, mind, and will is still what God calls us to, and the stakes for us and our children are just as high.

If we are honest, I think most parents would admit that they struggle to maintain and model this kind of devotion. In fact, we fail much of the time. Our falling short is not an indictment, judgment, or sentence. It's a line in the sand. However, if we can look in the mirror, are honest, and deeply consider the implications of our failures, we can begin at once to move in the right direction. We can always make the next right decision no matter where things are at this moment. What won't work is trying to stuff spiritual nourishment into our kids that we aren't partaking of ourselves. We can go online or visit a Christian bookstore to find all kinds of spiritual resources for our kids, but if we aren't going to live out our faith, it's not going to amount to anything.

Sobering Up

I feel the weight of these words as I write them. And I also feel caught in the tension of two competing desires. On the one hand, I want to provide encouraging words so that this reading or listening experience is a good one. On the other hand, I'm deeply saddened by research data indicating that in many ways the Western church is in trouble. It's hard to be encouraging when faced with the fact that fewer than one in ten young adults mention their faith as a top priority in their lives even though the vast majority of them were raised in church.[15]

It's a sobering time for faith, and yet this transitional season with all its harsh statistics is what needs to happen. It's time to be gut-wrenchingly honest about how committed we are to our faith — a faith contained in *the Bible*. I know of no more compelling reason to offer the Bible a significant place in our lives and families than this: it is the promise of our future.

In the midst of all the disconcerting data about the state of the church, I do see a ray of hope. Those who are young adults starting families right now say that they value family above all else.[16] This means that a generation that has spent time wandering is now turning toward home. Young adults are beginning to see that the grass is not greener on the other side; it's actually an arid desert — a spiritual desert not unlike the one in which the children of Israel wandered thousands of years ago. This is a generation that refuses to settle for anything less than authenticity and transparency in their faith. They want what they believe to be what they live. This gives us cause for hope, but we can't stop here.

If we want our children to be interested in the Bible, we have to be interested in it ourselves. If we want our kids to learn to honor, love, and accept Jesus as Savior, we have to do the same. If we actually want the Christian life in our families we've heard rumors about but have rarely experienced, we will have to develop an intimacy with Scripture that we've never really been able to achieve before.

None of us has life all worked out, especially in the context of family. When we read through the Scriptures in their context, we encounter amazing stories of heroic figures like King David, who actually failed at parenting and at transferring the treasure of his faith to all his children. This isn't a new struggle for parents. Perhaps your children are grown now and there is regret about the paths they've chosen. I wish I had been significantly more intentional about my faith as a younger man. I would have parented differently; I would have done most things differently. It is not possible to rewind life, but it is completely possible to alter the trajectory of where our lives are headed. It doesn't matter where you are now; there is always an opportunity to commit to a God-honoring path. There is time and there is grace. Begin now.

If this chapter has been a bit of a rough patch in an otherwise encouraging read and if you are sensing the Holy Spirit inviting you to consider deeply what's been said, I invite you to pray the prayer of recommitment for parents that I've included here.

Heavenly Father,

It is our deepest desire to introduce our children and our entire families to the truth of your Word. More importantly, it is our heart's desire to fling open the doors and windows of our homes to you. We know this begins with us.

Come, Holy Spirit. We invite you into the attics and corners, the closets and basements of our very souls. Nothing is off limits to you. We invite you to shine the light of truth into every area of our lives. Create in us a clean heart and renew a right spirit within us that we may serve you well. Guide us in the coming days so we can introduce our children to your ways and show them what a true relationship with you looks like. Help us to create a passion for your Word in our families by having such a passion in our own hearts.

By the authority of the work of Jesus we now take authority in our homes and reject anything there that does not honor you. We commit our children to you. We commit our relationships to you. We bow to your authority by giving you your rightful place at the center of our lives.

This we pray in the mighty and victorious name of Jesus our Savior.

                    Amen.

CHAPTER 9

FINDING YOUR PLACE
IN GOD'S STORY

Christ beside me, Christ before me, Christ behind me,
Christ within me, Christ beneath me, Christ above me.

— Saint Patrick

For this you and I were made, and this we must recover.

— John Eldredge

Just as you're insulting a good wine if you drink it from
a plastic cup instead of a glass which shows off its color,
bouquet, and full flavor, so you're insulting the Bible if,
given the opportunity, you don't create a context in
which it can be heard and celebrated as what it really is:
the rehearsal of the powerful deeds of God the creator
and rescuer.

— N. T. Wright

The most significant impact reading the Bible every day has had on me is discovering how relevant the Scripture is to whatever I need each day. I face struggles in almost every aspect of my life and when I read about the similar struggles of the Israelites, in the parables of Jesus, the passion of the Psalms or the wisdom of the Proverbs, it seems to put everything into focus. Each day, something strikes a chord and I have a "God Moment." Suddenly it's like God is speaking to me, revealing how, in the midst of whatever my predicament is, he is shaping me and building my character. I sometimes have a hard time seeing it in the moment, but when I can slow down and reflect on the words of Scripture, it starts to become clear. It's that clarity through the Scriptures that keeps me connected to God and helps me to put every aspect of my life back into focus.

— David, from Lincoln, Nebraska

Finding your place in God's story means listening with the ears of your heart and living life in the poetic rather than the purely rational. As odd as it seems in current culture, reason hasn't always been the primary approach to faith. Certainly the Age of Enlightenment brought Western civilization giant strides forward in many ways, but in the process we also lost some things, including a sense of won-der, or a more poetic experience of faith.

To find enrichment from Scripture while participating in an authentic relationship with God, we must reclaim this aspect of our faith. We can't force the deepest of spiritual matters to submit to the will of reason without doing vio-lence to them; this is not how faith operates.

The writer of Hebrews declares, "Faith is confidence in what we hope for and assurance about what we do not see" (Hebrews 11:1). Faith includes more than the rational mind alone can perceive. To get a clearer picture of this, let's con-sider the example of human attraction seen purely through the lens of science and reason.

When we are drawn to someone and are near to them, we have a physical reaction: our body pumps more adrenaline into the bloodstream, increasing our heart rate. We start to sweat. Our neurotransmitters are flooded with dopamine, giving us a sense of desire and the promise of pleasure. The response is so powerful it causes a brain reaction that's been likened to snorting cocaine. Our serotonin levels are impacted, and we can't get the person we love out of our minds. Even our sleep patterns are affected. I could go on describing the impact of other chemicals like oxytocin and vasopressin, but you're getting the idea, right? This is how science — the purely rational mind — might describe the phenomenon of attraction and love. It's an accurate sum-mary, but does it do justice to what is *really* going on inside us? Is that all there is to it?

Consider another example. What about the experience of betrayal? You know, the quick gasp for air that occurs when the shock hits? The awareness that everything you thought was true about a relationship was actually not true at all? You're trying simultaneously to understand what happened and to insulate yourself from the pain of it all. Nothing makes sense.

In the midst of this experience, how consoled would you be if your best friend were to sit with you and describe the cocktail of hormones and conflicting biochemicals driving all of your emotions? If your friend suggested drinking a glass of water and going for a jog so you could sweat out all the chemicals, do you think that would make the sting of betrayal go away? Of course not; the torture and chaos of betrayal can't be addressed at merely a biological level, nor can you cope with it through reason alone. You have a broken heart. Saying you have a broken heart is true, but it's not a statement that science alone would ever make. To capture the totality of the experience, you have to use a metaphor, a kind of emotional poetry that encompasses more than the rational mind can express.

In order to locate ourselves in God's story, we have to place reason in its proper position and give faith its rightful place. We have to look at the world through the eyes of the poetic by embracing more than reason. We must be open to things like art to capture and express what is otherwise inarticulate about our experience of God. This is where God resides, and by faith he's given us an amazing bridge to himself through one of the most powerful forces in the universe.

Let's look through the eyes of the poetic at what it's like to find ourselves in God's story.

Imagine

One of the ways we can find ourselves in God's story is to match biblical truths with prayerful imagination. Take, for example, the promise of peace that God gives us in many places throughout Scripture. The prophet Isaiah wrote, "You will keep in perfect peace those whose minds are steadfast, because they trust in you" (Isaiah 26:3). Rationally, we can affirm this truth but still find ourselves full of anxiety and fear. What does it mean to locate ourselves in God's story, which is rich with promises of peace? We can begin by imagining an experience of peace.

Imagine peace. No, actually stop reading and imagine it.

How would you describe peace? What does it look like for you? A deep breath and the slow exhale? Letting go of the anxieties and distractions that keep you running endlessly? Freedom from strife or dissension? That one place of tranquility and serenity? The kind of peace the prophet Isaiah described is a perfect peace. It is not hurried. It doesn't have a compulsive sense of low dose anxiety beneath everything as a base layer. Can you imagine what it would actually feel like to live this way?

It might be something like a couple quietly enjoying a leisurely picnic high in an alpine meadow. The scenery is beautiful, the wine is smooth and rich, the cheese aged to perfection, and the love between them waltzing in time with possibility. She speaks; he takes a moment and looks to the distant peaks for a response. He answers. She smiles. Silence. Minutes pass, but minutes do not exist, for this is not about getting anywhere. Accomplishment isn't the point. She gives, he receives and gives back — all in the gentle rhythms of uninterrupted conversation and time. No agendas, no plans other than that the moments pass as if they were limitless. Time spent as if there were an eternity of moments to generously spend.

There is a natural rhythm in this scene, and it is delicious to us because for a brief moment we've encountered a transcendent give and take. But it's everywhere. It's the rhythm of life. The call and response, the speaking and listening, the questioning and reflecting. This is how we communicate — with people we love and with God.

The first time I heard God specifically through the Scripture was June 25, 1996. I was a young Christian at the time, and my husband and I had started to read the Bible. He was traveling to his new six-month duty station at Khobar Towers in Saudi Arabia. I knew he had a layover in Frankfurt, but his actual time schedule was classified so I wasn't sure if he had arrived or was still in transit.

When I heard on CNN that the Khobar Towers had been bombed, and there were 15 known dead and 375 wounded, I gasped in disbelief. I tried to appear calm as I went through the normal routine of putting the children down for their afternoon nap, but I felt overwhelmed by fear. I got out a children's devotional book and read the kids to sleep as I had been doing for the past several months. The verses I read in the devotional nearly took my breath away and I read it aloud with tears in my eyes: "You will keep in perfect peace him whose mind is steadfast, because he trusts in you. Trust in the LORD forever, for the LORD, the LORD himself, is the Rock eternal" (Isaiah 26:3–4).

Peace rushed over me, and I felt sure that my husband was safe. I still nervously listened for the doorbell and paced in front of the TV as I prayed for all the people involved, not knowing how many of them my husband knew and where he actually was. Then the mailman came and there was a card from my husband saying that they had been delayed in Frankfurt and would be there for a whole week! According to my calculations, that meant he was still in Germany at the time of the bombing. A note in the card said, "I ran across this verse in my reading and think we should hold on to it while we are apart as a symbol of our strength from the Lord." It was Isaiah 26:3–4, the same verses I had just read to my children. Some may say it was a coincidence, but I felt God speak to me in a very real way.

—Gail, from Keller, Texas

Let's try the poetic approach again. A foundational truth of Scripture is God's love: "We know and rely on the love God has for us. God is love." (1 John 4:16a). Slow down and ponder this truth for a moment: God loves you. Even now, seeing that you're almost at the end of the book and can perhaps get it complete before the next task comes on the radar, do you find yourself eager to just keep racing ahead rather than pausing to really consider the truth of God's love?

Take a moment for real this time and locate yourself in this profound aspect of God's story. God truly and deeply loves you.

God deeply loves us like the couple picnicking in the alpine meadow love each other. He delights in us (Psalm 149:4). Look around you. What do you see? What sights remind you of God's love for you — of being quietly in God's presence? Is there a sunset? Enjoy its richness — the lavenders and peach, the fantastic sweeps of ginger and gold on a gradient of deepest indigo. Watch as the heavens beyond begin to twinkle; the evening coming to rest as the night watch begins. Smell the fresh-cut wheat from golden fields of plenty.

Are there sounds that usher you into God's love and care for you? When you listen to the fiddle and pipes play an ancient Irish lullaby as your little one's eyes slowly close for the night in perfect trust, do you hear God's invitation for you to rest in him? Can you imagine yourself embraced by God?

The chaos of contemporary life has us dulled to the point where we can hardly feel the beating of our hearts any longer. But this is not what we were made for. We were made for peace. We were meant for God. And we experience the truth of who God made us to be when we match biblical truth with a poetic and prayerful imagination.

Slow to the Beat
of the Father's Heart

One year I took a ride south along Highway 1 in Oregon with the Pacific Ocean as a traveling companion. It was grey and raining. South of Coos Bay I found what I was hoping for — miles of empty beach. The rain gave no indication of mercy, so embracing it I hiked the quarter mile down the sand embankment and across a field of huge and slippery drift logs. The ocean had dragged monstrous trees from some far off continent and beached them like a cat that drags a mouse to the front door, a prize for its master.

A few more paces down the coastal prairie path and I was on the open beach, walled in by massive rock formations rising from the ocean floor that captured and amplified her roar. It was loud enough that my fight or flee impulses were coming to life, and I fought the urge to turn and run. I was overcome by the sheer power of the waves. I felt like a speck, like one of the grains of sand. Facing the roar of the open sea, I had to bow to the creative force of God, who first conceived it and then spoke it into existence — a mere symbol of his glory and power.

I walked across a span of rocks that had been collected from all over the world and stored there — one of many treasuries of such wonders. A white piece of what appeared to be quartz stood out lying next to a small chunk of driftwood obviously deposited there with the last tide. A wave of heartache washed over me with the thought of my children, who were growing faster than I was comfortable with. It wasn't the kind of heartache that left me hopeless; it was the kind that any parent can relate to when considering what we have gained by becoming a father or mother and what we are losing by watching our children grow up. We are caretakers for but a moment, and then we hold our breath, cross our fingers, and breathe a fervent prayer as we watch them float away to write their own chapters on the tablets of history.

This is the kind of longing and profound love our heavenly Father feels for us. He creates a world for us, new every day, perhaps holding his breath and hoping to draw us closer to his heart. He leads and guides, but when all is said and done, we each choose freely where we will go. I have denied God in my life. I've questioned every value I was ever taught. I've resented. I've run. But time has allowed me to see that I was blaming God for everything I ever saw go wrong, heaping on him everything I could not explain on my own. It took years to realize that God wasn't behaving questionably. People were. I was. And God was watching the whole time, sending me love notes in a sunset or in an unexpected snow covering the Tennessee hill country. I would have never understood this without the Bible. Never. I would have been picked up by the tide once again and taken out to sea.

Becoming a parent has helped me understand a great deal about the depths of the Father's love for us. Somehow we just love this new little prince or princess with all the poopy diapers and baby puke. As they grow and develop a personality, we get an even better picture of how to raise them. But I can no more stop my children from making mistakes than I could freeze the ocean with a swipe of my hand. If I could mold their lives forcibly and craft them into what I thought they should be, I would miss the dynamic relationship that comes when a person has a free will.

And so it is in our relationship with God. *Why won't God speak more clearly to us?* we wonder. He is. He is always speaking to us, through everything, everywhere — and he's given us this book telling us the story of who we are and the enormous lengths he's been willing to go through to bring us back. Slow down and look around. God is calling your name.

There I was on that beach. No one else was around. The following day I'm sure the beach was different. Rocks moved, wood was dragged elsewhere, light and color changed, never to be exactly the same again. But right then, I was there to bear witness to what God had made, at that place, at that time. The moment was for me.

Where you stand at this precise moment is the only time in history that things will be as they are. This moment is for you. It is a gift from God. Don't let this pass you by.

Reversal

My lifestyle and passions have been utterly reversed because of my daily encounters with God through God's Word. My friendship with the Bible has taught me who my Father is and trained me to hear his voice. It has offered insight into what can be expected of me and ordered my days. Most important, it has given me hope. I didn't realize how dangerously I was living. I didn't realize I was on threadbare treads driving my life so carelessly in treacherous peril. I didn't even have a grid that would explain that there is an Evil One who would love to see that hope die along with me.

My desire is that somehow I've extended that hope to you and made an introduction to a dear and beloved friend of mine in God's Word. Be encouraged, my brother or sister. No matter what life looks like right at this moment, things are about to change. Not by magic but just the same they will most definitely change. Wherever you are and no matter your sense of distance from where you dream of being, this is the path. The Bible is the Word of God, and it will lead you to the life you were made for. King David said, "You make known to me the path of life; you will fill me with joy in your presence, with eternal pleasures at your right hand" (Psalm 16:11). Believe it. Begin now.

As I climbed back up the dunes and slumped into the driver's seat overlooking the endless Pacific, I felt immense gratitude. I felt that the moment must be carried forward in my heart always. I put the car in drive, but not to make time or burn miles; it was for the adventure of finding what was around the next bend. The ocean and the cliffs ahead in my journey will combine to make something only worthy of an awesome, creative God, a warrior God who would travel across universes and all eternity to make every light and every shadow a perfect one to experience.

How deep the Father's love for us
How vast beyond all measure.[17]

NO JOKE, YOU WILL NEVER BE THE SAME

I t's an autumn morning in the rolling hills of Tennessee where I live hidden away from most of the sprawl of a city that seems intent on slowly claiming every open space in the years to come. The story of writing this book is a long enough one to fill many, many pages all on its own, but it would be nearly impossible to tell the story anyway because so much of it can't be transferred to paper. The real story is in the changes of mind, heart, and will that happen each day as age and experience collide with the bedrock of biblical truth. Reading the Bible has changed me — and it can do the same for you.

This is a promise. You won't be the same after reading the Bible every day for a year. Immersing yourself in the truth of God's Word will make you different. So what are you waiting for? Go for it!

There is nothing that I believe will create the change we want to see in the world more than if God's people will read

God's Word every day and be transformed by the power contained within it. At the same time I know how easy it's going to be to "westernize" what that change is supposed to look like, and so I want to leave you with a few words of counsel.

Guidelines to Get You Started

Embrace the whole truth. Resist the temptation to approach Scripture with a "pick and choose" mindset. It won't work, and you will not experience the kind of change you hope for. Allow the whole truth of the Bible to access your life by accepting that all of it is the revealed Word of God.

Expect to be challenged. The Bible isn't a surface document. It won't be content to merely sweep the floors of your life and tidy up a bit. It's going to challenge you to face up to some of the attitudes, beliefs, and behaviors that have landed you in heaps of trouble along the way. It's going to ask you to step down willingly off the throne of your life, to allow God to assume that place, and to invite you to bow down to his authority. Sooner or later, you will be asked to die to yourself, which is no easy thing.

Persevere. When the challenge comes, don't give up. Stay with it. Press into it. Do not falter. You have the choice about who you will be in a year. Submitting yourself to the disciplines and obedience demanded in Scripture builds strength and provides life-giving boundaries. These boundaries aren't there to cage you; they are there to save you, to give a set of parameters that will provide ultimate freedom and fulfillment.

Make the Bible plan A (not plan B). When life pulls the rug out from under us and we find ourselves alone and flat on the floor, we like to swiftly dust off the Bible and start talking to God as if we've been best buds all this time and he probably didn't even notice we'd been gone or what we'd been up to.

This doesn't work.

I say this with the conviction of a person who absolutely knows it to be true. If we were having a conversation, I would be looking you straight in the eye. The Bible is not a spiritual safety net or an insurance policy in the way we traditionally think of such things. It's not the place to crash and reorient until we can return to our own style of crisis management. It's not a crutch to hobble forward on until we can get back on our feet and desert his Word again.

We have to be willing to give our hearts to God fully. God withheld nothing from us when he sent his Son, and he will accept nothing less in return. This isn't a big cliché pitch to surrender your life fully to Christ; the trade is so lopsided, it's almost laughable. The Sovereign Lord offers us eternal and everlasting life in his presence in exchange for whatever it is we are at whatever moment we give up on being our own lord and god and simply let go. God will rescue us and his Word will be a huge part of that story, but God — and the Bible — must be plan A.

How Different Is Different?

I recently watched "Whale Wars" with my wife and daughter. In this program a rag-tag group of conservationists band together with a couple of old ships to sail into the Antarctic during whaling season and do everything they possibly can to disrupt the Japanese from killing whales under the pretense of scientific research. The lengths in which they will go to confront what they see as an unforgiveable injustice are what create the drama for the program. It's easy to look at these people trying to save dolphins and whales as whacko environmentalists, but it's difficult to dismiss their passion for and commitment to what they think is right.

I found myself staring at the ceiling as I lay in bed one evening and couldn't get these people out of my mind. They were truly willing to put their lives in jeopardy. They left nice homes and steady jobs and gave up most comforts to live very lean and simply. They basically lived semi-monastic lives without the prayer. They lived more Christ-like in actual practice than most Western Christians. They were passionate enough about what they believed in to look absolutely foolish and wear whatever label society chose to give them in order to achieve what they believed to be a just cause.

This is the kind of commitment the Bible invites us into and a glimpse of what it means to be a committed disciple of Christ. It would look pretty much as it did when the twelve ragamuffin disciples were following their controversial and countercultural rabbi around Judea. This ends up being a lot less like the trendy, normal American who happens to have a little religion and more like one of those fully committed people saving whales or dolphins who are willing to be marginalized if that's what it takes.

If we are living truly free, awake, and alert to the truth — and completely disinterested in the distractions, addictions, or other false constructs that try to pass themselves off as life — we will in fact be free, but we will also probably look increasingly strange and peculiar to those around us (see 1 Peter 2:9; Titus 2:14 KJV).

Saying this is my way of offering full disclosure. You won't be the same after the Bible. You won't care about some of the things you care a lot about now. Some of the things that seem huge in life at the moment are going to simply not matter this time next year. It's true that the stresses and distractions of life will be forced into their proper perspective, but the Bible will never offer the comfort of complacency. It will never allow stagnation. It will never allow us to depend on ourselves and create alternative plans that get things done without God anymore. That isn't life.

The Bible is about becoming more like Christ. It constantly invites us to submit ourselves in obedience not to make us miserable but to change us from the inside out. An authentic relationship with Jesus is an all-or-nothing proposition, and this requires change. Some changes will likely come hard. It's not easy to untangle all the kudzu that's been growing around our hearts and minds as we've done our best to make life work on our own terms. It's not particularly pleasant to allow the Holy Spirit to move into the wounded places in our lives and begin to truly heal what has been oozing bitterness and disappointment.

None of this comes easily, but you don't have to do it alone. God's Word is the friend you have needed all along, and in cooperation with the Holy Spirit (John 16:7), you will never walk alone (Matthew 28:20).

Prepare Yourself

Go look in the mirror. Look deeply into your eyes. After journeying through the Bible every day for a year, I'd love for you to return to the mirror. You're likely to see new life twinkling from behind those eyes that isn't there right now. Those stresses and worries that are pulling at you aren't going to be the giants they can seem to be these days. You're going to be different. You will have been transformed from the inside out, but you won't likely get there by any of the roads you've ever traveled before. This is the beauty of being in love, and this is the adventure of traveling with one who knows where all the hidden and breathtaking vistas are.

May you find life in God's Word, my friend, and may true life find you. May the Lord bless you and keep you. May he make his face to shine upon you and be gracious to you. May he lift up his countenance on you and give you peace. May the strength of God go with you. May the wisdom of God instruct you. May the hand of God protect you. May the Word of God direct you.

May you be sealed in Christ this day and forevermore. Amen.

Brian Hardin
May 21, 2011
Spring Hill, Tennessee

NOTES

1. www.gallup.com/poll/27682/OneThird-Americans-Believe-Bible
   -Literally-True.aspx (accessed May 12, 2011).
2. http://wiki.answers.com/Q/What_percentage_of_people_read
   _the_bible (accessed May 12, 2011).
3. www.theologicalstudies.org/page/page/1572910.htm (accessed May
   12, 2011).
4. www.catholicnews.com/data/stories/cns/0802435.htm (accessed
   May 12, 2011).
5. Used by permission.
6. Meditating on God's Word is a practice evident throughout the
   pages of Scripture. See Joshua 1:8; Psalms 1:2; 4:4; 63:6; 77:11–12;
   78:42; 143:5; 145:5; Isaiah 55:8–9; Luke 2:19; Philippians 4:8.
7. www.ethnologue.com/ethno_docs/distribution.asp?by=area
   (accessed May 17, 2011).
8. http://wiki.answers.com/Q/How_many_different_dialects_are
   _there_in_the_world (accessed May 17, 2011).
9. http://portal.unesco.org/education/en/ev.php-URL_
   ID=28301&URL_DO=DO_TOPIC&URL_SECTION=201.html
   (accessed May 17, 2011).
10. http://itre.cis.upenn.edu/~myl/languagelog/archives/003420.html
    (accessed May 17, 2011).
11. www.biblica.com/bibles/about/19.php (accessed May 17, 2011).
12. www.pbs.org/wgbh/nova/bible/written.html (accessed May 17, 2011).)
13. www.pbs.org/wgbh/nova/bible/written.html (accessed May 17, 2011).
14. http://en.wikipedia.org/wiki/Printing_press (accessed May 18, 2011).
15. www.unchristian.com/downloads2.asp (summary of the Barna
    Research contained in this book; accessed May 18, 2011).
16. www.lifeway.com/article/170251/ (accessed May 19, 2011).
17. Stuart Townsend ©1995 Thankyou Music (admin. by EMI Christian
    Music Publishing).

BIBLE READING PLANS

The Bible is a large book spanning thousands of years of history and events. It's history, it's spirituality, it's human, and yet it transcends humanity to the very essence of who we are and who God is. It's beyond epic for God creates, human race falls, God comes in the flesh to restore humanity, and everything changes. Then there are the stories and letters of how the church was formed and went about continuing the work of Jesus. There are many ways to approach Scripture. Here are a few suggestions and reading plans to guide your first revolution in a year.

The Daily Audio Bible Reading Plan

This reading plan is what we use as we go through the Bible in community each year. It allows us to move through the Old and New Testaments simultaneously. In many cases it shows something beginning in the Old Testament and being fulfilled in the New. It also keeps things dynamic. The stories of the genealogies in the Old Testament are vitally important to the historical record, but they are not particularly staggering reading material. This plan allows us to work through these portions and give them space to breathe because we're also working through other portions of Scripture. There is essentially one psalm per day and some spice from the Proverbs, which will often say in one sentence something you will not stop thinking about for an entire day. This reading plan is available as an eBible also called *Passages* and is the companion to this book.

I recommend you take your first journey through the Bible this way.

DAY	DATE	SCRIPTURE
1	**January 1**	Genesis 1:1 – 2:25; Matthew 1:1 – 2:12; Psalm 1:1 – 6; Proverbs 1:1 – 6
2	**January 2**	Genesis 3:1 – 4:26; Matthew 2:13 – 3:6; Psalm 2:1 – 12; Proverbs 1:7 – 9
3	**January 3**	Genesis 5:1 – 7:24; Matthew 3:7 – 4:11; Psalm 3:1 – 8; Proverbs 1:10 – 19
4	**January 4**	Genesis 8:1 – 10:32; Matthew 4:12 – 25; Psalm 4:1 – 8; Proverbs 1:20 – 23
5	**January 5**	Genesis 11:1 – 13:4; Matthew 5:1 – 26; Psalm 5:1 – 12; Proverbs 1:24 – 28
6	**January 6**	Genesis 13:5 – 15:21; Matthew 5:27 – 48; Psalm 6:1 – 10; Proverbs 1:29 – 33

THE DAILY AUDIO BIBLE READING PLAN

DAY	DATE	SCRIPTURE
7	January 7	Genesis 16:1–18:15; Matthew 6:1–24; Psalm 7:1–17; Proverbs 2:1–5
8	January 8	Genesis 18:16–19:38; Matthew 6:25–7:14; Psalm 8:1–9; Proverbs 2:6–15
9	January 9	Genesis 20:1–22:24; Matthew 7:15–29; Psalm 9:1–12; Proverbs 2:16–22
10	January 10	Genesis 23:1–24:51; Matthew 8:1–17; Psalm 9:13–20; Proverbs 3:1–6
11	January 11	Genesis 24:52–26:16; Matthew 8:18–34; Psalm 10:1–15; Proverbs 3:7–8
12	January 12	Genesis 26:17–27:46; Matthew 9:1–17; Psalm 10:16–18; Proverbs 3:9–10
13	January 13	Genesis 28:1–29:35; Matthew 9:18–38; Psalm 11:1–7; Proverbs 3:11–12
14	January 14	Genesis 30:1–31:16; Matthew 10:1–23; Psalm 12:1–8; Proverbs 3:13–15
15	January 15	Genesis 31:17–32:12; Matthew 10:24–11:6; Psalm 13:1–6; Proverbs 3:16–18
16	January 16	Genesis 32:13–34:31; Matthew 11:7–30; Psalm 14:1–7; Proverbs 3:19–20
17	January 17	Genesis 35:1–36:43; Matthew 12:1–21; Psalm 15:1–5; Proverbs 3:21–26
18	January 18	Genesis 37:1–38:30; Matthew 12:22–45; Psalm 16:1–11; Proverbs 3:27–32
19	January 19	Genesis 39:1–41:16; Matthew 12:46–13:23; Psalm 17:1–15; Proverbs 3:33–35
20	January 20	Genesis 41:17–42:17; Matthew 13:24–46; Psalm 18:1–15; Proverbs 4:1–6
21	January 21	Genesis 42:18–43:34; Matthew 13:47–14:12 Psalm 18:16–36; Proverbs 4:7–10
22	January 22	Genesis 44:1–45:28; Matthew 14:13–36; Psalm 18:37–50; Proverbs 4:11–13

BIBLE READING PLANS

DAY	DATE	SCRIPTURE
23	January 23	Genesis 46:1–47:31; Matthew 15:1–28; Psalm 19:1–14; Proverbs 4:14–19
24	January 24	Genesis 48:1–49:33; Matthew 15:29–16:12; Psalm 20:1–9; Proverbs 4:20–27
25	January 25	Genesis 50:1–Exodus 2:10; Matthew 16:13–17:9; Psalm 21:1–13; Proverbs 5:1–6
26	January 26	Exodus 2:11–3:22; Matthew 17:10–27; Psalm 22:1–18; Proverbs 5:7–14
27	January 27	Exodus 4:1–5:21; Matthew 18:1–20; Psalm 22:19–31; Proverbs 5:15–21
28	January 28	Exodus 5:22–7:24; Matthew 18:21–19:12; Psalm 23:1–6; Proverbs 5:22–23
29	January 29	Exodus 7:25–9:35; Matthew 19:13–30; Psalm 24:1–10; Proverbs 6:1–5
30	January 30	Exodus 10:1–12:13; Matthew 20:1–28; Psalm 25:1–11; Proverbs 6:6–11
31	January 31	Exodus 12:14–13:16; Matthew 20:29–21:22; Psalm 25:12–22; Proverbs 6:12–15
32	February 1	Exodus 13:17–15:18; Matthew 21:23–46; Psalm 26:1–12; Proverbs 6:16–19
33	February 2	Exodus 15:19–17:7; Matthew 22:1–33; Psalm 27:1–7; Proverbs 6:20–26
34	February 3	Exodus 17:8–19:15; Matthew 22:34–23:12; Psalm 27:8–14; Proverbs 6:27–35
35	February 4	Exodus 19:16–21:21; Matthew 23:13–39; Psalm 28:1–9; Proverbs 7:1–5
36	February 5	Exodus 21:22–23:13; Matthew 24:1–28; Psalm 29:1–11; Proverbs 7:6–23
37	February 6	Exodus 23:14–25:40; Matthew 24:29–51; Psalm 30:1–12; Proverbs 7:24–27
38	February 7	Exodus 26:1–27:21; Matthew 25:1–30; Psalm 31:1–8; Proverbs 8:1–11

THE DAILY AUDIO BIBLE READING PLAN

DAY	DATE	SCRIPTURE
39	**February 8**	Exodus 28:1 – 43; Matthew 25:31 – 26:13; Psalm 31:9 – 18; Proverbs 8:12 – 13
40	**February 9**	Exodus 29:1 – 30:10; Matthew 26:14 – 46; Psalm 31:19 – 24; Proverbs 8:14 – 26
41	**February 10**	Exodus 30:11 – 31:18; Matthew 26:47 – 68; Psalm 32:1 – 11; Proverbs 8:27 – 32
42	**February 11**	Exodus 32:1 – 33:23; Matthew 26:69 – 27:14; Psalm 33:1 – 11; Proverbs 8:33 – 36
43	**February 12**	Exodus 34:1 – 35:9; Matthew 27:15 – 31; Psalm 33:12 – 22; Proverbs 9:1 – 6
44	**February 13**	Exodus 35:10 – 36:38; Matthew 27:32 – 66; Psalm 34:1 – 10; Proverbs 9:7 – 8
45	**February 14**	Exodus 37:1 – 38:31; Matthew 28:1 – 20; Psalm 34:11 – 22; Proverbs 9:9 – 10
46	**February 15**	Exodus 39:1 – 40:38; Mark 1:1 – 28; Psalm 35:1 – 16; Proverbs 9:11 – 12
47	**February 16**	Leviticus 1:1 – 3:17; Mark 1:29 – 2:12; Psalm 35:17 – 28; Proverbs 9:13 – 18
48	**February 17**	Leviticus 4:1 – 5:19; Mark 2:13 – 3:6; Psalm 36:1 – 12; Proverbs 10:1 – 2
49	**February 18**	Leviticus 6:1 – 7:27; Mark 3:7 – 30; Psalm 37:1 – 11; Proverbs 10:3 – 4
50	**February 19**	Leviticus 7:28 – 9:6; Mark 3:31 – 4:25; Psalm 37:12 – 29; Proverbs 10:5
51	**February 20**	Leviticus 9:7 – 10:20; Mark 4:26 – 5:20; Psalm 37:30 – 40; Proverbs 10:6 – 7
52	**February 21**	Leviticus 11:1 – 12:8; Mark 5:21 – 43; Psalm 38:1 – 22; Proverbs 10:8 – 9
53	**February 22**	Leviticus 13:1 – 59; Mark 6:1 – 29; Psalm 39:1 – 13; Proverbs 10:10
54	**February 23**	Leviticus 14:1 – 57; Mark 6:30 – 56; Psalm 40:1 – 10; Proverbs 10:11 – 12

BIBLE READING PLANS

DAY	DATE	SCRIPTURE
55	**February 24**	Leviticus 15:1 – 16:28; Mark 7:1 – 23; Psalm 40:11 – 17; Proverbs 10:13 – 14
56	**February 25**	Leviticus 16:29 – 18:30; Mark 7:24 – 8:10; Psalm 41:1 – 13; Proverbs 10:15 – 16
57	**February 26**	Leviticus 19:1 – 20:21; Mark 8:11 – 38; Psalm 42:1 – 11; Proverbs 10:17
58	**February 27**	Leviticus 20:22 – 22:16; Mark 9:1 – 29; Psalm 43:1 – 5; Proverbs 10:18
59	**February 28**	Leviticus 22:17 – 23:44; Mark 9:30 – 10:12; Psalm 44:1 – 8; Proverbs 10:19
60	**March 1**	Leviticus 24:1 – 25:46; Mark 10:13 – 31; Psalm 44:9 – 26; Proverbs 10:20 – 21
61	**March 2**	Leviticus 25:47 – 27:13; Mark 10:32 – 52; Psalm 45:1 – 17; Proverbs 10:22
62	**March 3**	Leviticus 27:14 – Numbers 1:54; Mark 11:1 – 26; Psalm 46:1 – 11; Proverbs 10:23
63	**March 4**	Numbers 2:1 – 3:51; Mark 11:27 – 12:17; Psalm 47:1 – 9; Proverbs 10:24 – 25
64	**March 5**	Numbers 4:1 – 5:31; Mark 12:18 – 37; Psalm 48:1 – 14; Proverbs 10:26
65	**March 6**	Numbers 6:1 – 7:89; Mark 12:38 – 13:13; Psalm 49:1 – 20; Proverbs 10:27 – 28
66	**March 7**	Numbers 8:1 – 9:23; Mark 13:14 – 37; Psalm 50:1 – 23; Proverbs 10:29 – 30
67	**March 8**	Numbers 10:1 – 11:23; Mark 14:1 – 21; Psalm 51:1 – 19; Proverbs 10:31 – 32
68	**March 9**	Numbers 11:24 – 13:33; Mark 14:22 – 52; Psalm 52:1 – 9; Proverbs 11:1 – 3
69	**March 10**	Numbers 14:1 – 15:16; Mark 14:53 – 72; Psalm 53:1 – 6; Proverbs 11:4
70	**March 11**	Numbers 15:17 – 16:40; Mark 15:1 – 47; Psalm 54:1 – 7; Proverbs 11:5 – 6

THE DAILY AUDIO BIBLE READING PLAN

DAY	DATE	SCRIPTURE
71	March 12	Numbers 16:41 – 18:32; Mark 16:1 – 20; Psalm 55:1 – 23; Proverbs 11:7
72	March 13	Numbers 19:1 – 20:29; Luke 1:1 – 25; Psalm 56:1 – 13; Proverbs 11:8
73	March 14	Numbers 21:1 – 22:20; Luke 1:26 – 56; Psalm 57:1 – 11; Proverbs 11:9 – 11
74	March 15	Numbers 22:21 – 23:30; Luke 1:57 – 80; Psalm 58:1 – 11; Proverbs 11:12 – 13
75	March 16	Numbers 24:1 – 25:18; Luke 2:1 – 35; Psalm 59:1 – 17; Proverbs 11:14
76	March 17	Numbers 26:1 – 51; Luke 2:36 – 52; Psalm 60:1 – 12; Proverbs 11:15
77	March 18	Numbers 26:52 – 28:15; Luke 3:1 – 22; Psalm 61:1 – 8; Proverbs 11:16 – 17
78	March 19	Numbers 28:16 – 29:40; Luke 3:23 – 38; Psalm 62:1 – 12; Proverbs 11:18 – 19
79	March 20	Numbers 30:1 – 31:54; Luke 4:1 – 30; Psalm 63:1 – 11; Proverbs 11:20 – 21
80	March 21	Numbers 32:1 – 33:39; Luke 4:31 – 5:11; Psalm 64:1 – 10; Proverbs 11:22
81	March 22	Numbers 33:40 – 35:34; Luke 5:12 – 39; Psalm 65:1 – 13; Proverbs 11:23
82	March 23	Numbers 36:1 – Deuteronomy 1:46; Luke 6:1 – 11; Psalm 66:1 – 20; Proverbs 11:24 – 26
83	March 24	Deuteronomy 2:1 – 3:29; Luke 6:12 – 38; Psalm 67:1 – 7; Proverbs 11:27
84	March 25	Deuteronomy 4:1 – 49; Luke 6:39 – 7:10; Psalm 68:1 – 18; Proverbs 11:28
85	March 26	Deuteronomy 5:1 – 6:25; Luke 7:11 – 35; Psalm 68:19 – 35; Proverbs 11:29 – 31
86	March 27	Deuteronomy 7:1 – 8:20; Luke 7:36 – 8:3; Psalm 69:1 – 18; Proverbs 12:1

BIBLE READING PLANS

DAY	DATE	SCRIPTURE
87	March 28	Deuteronomy 9:1 – 10:22; Luke 8:4 – 21; Psalm 69:19 – 36; Proverbs 12:2 – 3
88	March 29	Deuteronomy 11:1 – 12:32; Luke 8:22 – 39; Psalm 70:1 – 5; Proverbs 12:4
89	March 30	Deuteronomy 13:1 – 15:23; Luke 8:40 – 9:6; Psalm 71:1 – 24; Proverbs 12:5 – 7
90	March 31	Deuteronomy 16:1 – 17:20; Luke 9:7 – 27; Psalm 72:1 – 20; Proverbs 12:8 – 9
91	April 1	Deuteronomy 18:1 – 20:20; Luke 9:28 – 50; Psalm 73:1 – 28; Proverbs 12:10
92	April 2	Deuteronomy 21:1 – 22:30; Luke 9:51 – 10:12; Psalm 74:1 – 23; Proverbs 12:11
93	April 3	Deuteronomy 23:1 – 25:19; Luke 10:13 – 37; Psalm 75:1 – 10; Proverbs 12:12 – 14
94	April 4	Deuteronomy 26:1 – 27:26; Luke 10:38 – 11:13; Psalm 76:1 – 12; Proverbs 12:15 – 17
95	April 5	Deuteronomy 28:1 – 68; Luke 11:14 – 36; Psalm 77:1 – 20; Proverbs 12:18
96	April 6	Deuteronomy 29:1 – 30:20; Luke 11:37 – 12:7; Psalm 78:1 – 31; Proverbs 12:19 – 20
97	April 7	Deuteronomy 31:1 – 32:27; Luke 12:8 – 34; Psalm 78:32 – 55; Proverbs 12:21 – 23
98	April 8	Deuteronomy 32:28 – 52; Luke 12:35 – 59; Psalm 78:56 – 64; Proverbs 12:24
99	April 9	Deuteronomy 33:1 – 29; Luke 13:1 – 21; Psalm 78:65 – 72; Proverbs 12:25
100	April 10	Deuteronomy 34:1 – Joshua 2:24; Luke 13:22 – 14:6; Psalm 79:1 – 13; Proverbs 12:26
101	April 11	Joshua 3:1 – 4:24; Luke 14:7 – 35; Psalm 80:1 – 19; Proverbs 12:27 – 28
102	April 12	Joshua 5:1 – 7:15; Luke 15:1 – 32; Psalm 81:1 – 16; Proverbs 13:1

THE DAILY AUDIO BIBLE READING PLAN

DAY	DATE	SCRIPTURE
103	April 13	Joshua 7:16 – 9:2; Luke 16:1 – 18; Psalm 82:1 – 8; Proverbs 13:2 – 3
104	April 14	Joshua 9:3 – 10:43; Luke 16:19 – 17:10; Psalm 83:1 – 18; Proverbs 13:4
105	April 15	Joshua 11:1 – 12:24; Luke 17:11 – 37; Psalm 84:1 – 12; Proverbs 13:5 – 6
106	April 16	Joshua 13:1 – 14:15; Luke 18:1 – 17; Psalm 85:1 – 13; Proverbs 13:7 – 8
107	April 17	Joshua 15:1 – 63; Luke 18:18 – 43; Psalm 86:1 – 17; Proverbs 13:9 – 10
108	April 18	Joshua 16:1 – 18:28; Luke 19:1 – 27; Psalm 87:1 – 7; Proverbs 13:11
109	April 19	Joshua 19:1 – 20:9; Luke 19:28 – 48; Psalm 88:1 – 18; Proverbs 13:12 – 14
110	April 20	Joshua 21:1 – 22:20; Luke 20:1 – 26; Psalm 89:1 – 13; Proverbs 13:15 – 16
111	April 21	Joshua 22:21 – 23:16; Luke 20:27 – 47; Psalm 89:14 – 37; Proverbs 13:17 – 19
112	April 22	Joshua 24:1 – 33; Luke 21:1 – 28; Psalm 89:38 – 52; Proverbs 13:20 – 23
113	April 23	Judges 1:1 – 2:9; Luke 21:29 – 22:13; Psalm 90:1 – 91:16; Proverbs 13:24 – 25
114	April 24	Judges 2:10 – 3:31; Luke 22:14 – 34; Psalm 92:1 – 93:5; Proverbs 14:1 – 2
115	April 25	Judges 4:1 – 5:31; Luke 22:35 – 53; Psalm 94:1 – 23; Proverbs 14:3 – 4
116	April 26	Judges 6:1 – 40; Luke 22:54 – 23:12; Psalm 95:1 – 96:13; Proverbs 14:5 – 6
117	April 27	Judges 7:1 – 8:17; Luke 23:13 – 43; Psalm 97:1 – 98:9; Proverbs 14:7 – 8
118	April 28	Judges 8:18 – 9:21; Luke 23:44 – 24:12; Psalm 99:1 – 9; Proverbs 14:9 – 10

BIBLE READING PLANS

DAY	DATE	SCRIPTURE
119	April 29	Judges 9:22–10:18; Luke 24:13–53; Psalm 100:1–5; Proverbs 14:11–12
120	April 30	Judges 11:1–12:15; John 1:1–28; Psalm 101:1–8; Proverbs 14:13–14
121	May 1	Judges 13:1–14:20; John 1:29–51; Psalm 102:1–28; Proverbs 14:15–16
122	May 2	Judges 15:1–16:31; John 2:1–25; Psalm 103:1–22; Proverbs 14:17–19
123	May 3	Judges 17:1–18:31; John 3:1–21; Psalm 104:1–23; Proverbs 14:20–21
124	May 4	Judges 19:1–20:48; John 3:22–4:3; Psalm 104:24–35; Proverbs 14:22–24
125	May 5	Judges 21:1–Ruth 1:22; John 4:4–42; Psalm 105:1–15; Proverbs 14:25
126	May 6	Ruth 2:1–4:22; John 4:43–54; Psalm 105:16–36; Proverbs 14:26–27
127	May 7	1 Samuel 1:1–2:21; John 5:1–23; Psalm 105:37–45; Proverbs 14:28–29
128	May 8	1 Samuel 2:22–4:22; John 5:24–47; Psalm 106:1–12; Proverbs 14:30–31
129	May 9	1 Samuel 5:1–7:17; John 6:1–21; Psalm 106:13–31; Proverbs 14:32–33
130	May 10	1 Samuel 8:1–9:27; John 6:22–42; Psalm 106:32–48; Proverbs 14:34–35
131	May 11	1 Samuel 10:1–11:15; John 6:43–71; Psalm 107:1–43; Proverbs 15:1–3
132	May 12	1 Samuel 12:1–13:23; John 7:1–30; Psalm 108:1–13; Proverbs 15:4
133	May 13	1 Samuel 14:1–52; John 7:31–53; Psalm 109:1–31; Proverbs 15:5–7
134	May 14	1 Samuel 15:1–16:23; John 8:1–20; Psalm 110:1–7; Proverbs 15:8–10

THE DAILY AUDIO BIBLE READING PLAN

DAY	DATE	SCRIPTURE
135	May 15	1 Samuel 17:1–18:4; John 8:21–30; Psalm 111:1–10; Proverbs 15:11
136	May 16	1 Samuel 18:5–19:24; John 8:31–59; Psalm 112:1–10; Proverbs 15:12–14
137	May 17	1 Samuel 20:1–21:15; John 9:1–41; Psalm 113:1–114:8; Proverbs 15:15–17
138	May 18	1 Samuel 22:1–23:29; John 10:1–21; Psalm 115:1–18; Proverbs 15:18–19
139	May 19	1 Samuel 24:1–25:44; John 10:22–42; Psalm 116:1–19; Proverbs 15:20–21
140	May 20	1 Samuel 26:1–28:25; John 11:1–54; Psalm 117:1–2; Proverbs 15:22–23
141	May 21	1 Samuel 29:1–31:13; John 11:55–12:19; Psalm 118:1–18; Proverbs 15:24–26
142	May 22	2 Samuel 1:1–2:11; John 12:20–50; Psalm 118:19–29; Proverbs 15:27–28
143	May 23	2 Samuel 2:12–3:39; John 13:1–30; Psalm 119:1–16; Proverbs 15:29–30
144	May 24	2 Samuel 4:1–6:23; John 13:31–14:14; Psalm 119:17–32; Proverbs 15:31–32
145	May 25	2 Samuel 7:1–8:18; John 14:15–31; Psalm 119:33–48; Proverbs 15:33
146	May 26	2 Samuel 9:1–11:27; John 15:1–27; Psalm 119:49–64; Proverbs 16:1–3
147	May 27	2 Samuel 12:1–31; John 16:1–33; Psalm 119:65–80; Proverbs 16:4–5
148	May 28	2 Samuel 13:1–39; John 17:1–26; Psalm 119:81–96; Proverbs 16:6–7
149	May 29	2 Samuel 14:1–15:22; John 18:1–24; Psalm 119:97–112; Proverbs 16:8–9
150	May 30	2 Samuel 15:23–16:23; John 18:25–19:22; Psalm 119:113–128; Proverbs 16:10–11

BIBLE READING PLANS

DAY	DATE	SCRIPTURE
151	May 31	2 Samuel 17:1–29; John 19:23–42; Psalm 119:129–152; Proverbs 16:12–13
152	June 1	2 Samuel 18:1–19:10; John 20:1–31; Psalm 119:153–176; Proverbs 16:14–15
153	June 2	2 Samuel 19:11–20:13; John 21:1–25; Psalm 120:1–7; Proverbs 16:16–17
154	June 3	2 Samuel 20:14–21:22; Acts 1:1–26; Psalm 121:1–8; Proverbs 16:18
155	June 4	2 Samuel 22:1–23:23; Acts 2:1–47; Psalm 122:1–9; Proverbs 16:19–20
156	June 5	2 Samuel 23:24–24:25; Acts 3:1–26; Psalm 123:1–4; Proverbs 16:21–23
157	June 6	1 Kings 1:1–53; Acts 4:1–37; Psalm 124:1–8; Proverbs 16:24
158	June 7	1 Kings 2:1–3:2; Acts 5:1–42; Psalm 125:1–5; Proverbs 16:25
159	June 8	1 Kings 3:3–4:34; Acts 6:1–15; Psalm 126:1–6; Proverbs 16:26–27
160	June 9	1 Kings 5:1–6:38; Acts 7:1–29; Psalm 127:1–5; Proverbs 16:28–30
161	June 10	1 Kings 7:1–51; Acts 7:30–50; Psalm 128:1–6; Proverbs 16:31–33
162	June 11	1 Kings 8:1–66; Acts 7:51–8:13; Psalm 129:1–8; Proverbs 17:1
163	June 12	1 Kings 9:1–10:29; Acts 8:14–40; Psalm 130:1–8; Proverbs 17:2–3
164	June 13	1 Kings 11:1–12:19; Acts 9:1–25; Psalm 131:1–3; Proverbs 17:4–5
165	June 14	1 Kings 12:20–13:34; Acts 9:26–43; Psalm 132:1–18; Proverbs 17:6
166	June 15	1 Kings 14:1–15:24; Acts 10:1–23; Psalm 133:1–3; Proverbs 17:7–8

THE DAILY AUDIO BIBLE READING PLAN

DAY	DATE	SCRIPTURE
167	June 16	1 Kings 15:25 – 17:24; Acts 10:24 – 48; Psalm 134:1 – 3; Proverbs 17:9 – 11
168	June 17	1 Kings 18:1 – 46; Acts 11:1 – 30; Psalm 135:1 – 21; Proverbs 17:12 – 13
169	June 18	1 Kings 19:1 – 21; Acts 12:1 – 23; Psalm 136:1 – 26; Proverbs 17:14 – 15
170	June 19	1 Kings 20:1 – 21:29; Acts 12:24 – 13:15; Psalm 137:1 – 9; Proverbs 17:16
171	June 20	1 Kings 22:1 – 53; Acts 13:16 – 41; Psalm 138:1 – 8; Proverbs 17:17 – 18
172	June 21	2 Kings 1:1 – 2:25; Acts 13:42 – 14:7; Psalm 139:1 – 24; Proverbs 17:19 – 21
173	June 22	2 Kings 3:1 – 4:17; Acts 14:8 – 28; Psalm 140:1 – 13; Proverbs 17:22
174	June 23	2 Kings 4:18 – 5:27; Acts 15:1 – 35; Psalm 141:1 – 10; Proverbs 17:23
175	June 24	2 Kings 6:1 – 7:20; Acts 15:36 – 16:15; Psalm 142:1 – 7; Proverbs 17:24 – 25
176	June 25	2 Kings 8:1 – 9:13; Acts 16:16 – 40; Psalm 143:1 – 12; Proverbs 17:26
177	June 26	2 Kings 9:14 – 10:31; Acts 17:1 – 34; Psalm 144:1 – 15; Proverbs 17:27 – 28
178	June 27	2 Kings 10:32 – 12:21; Acts 18:1 – 22; Psalm 145:1 – 21; Proverbs 18:1
179	June 28	2 Kings 13:1 – 14:29; Acts 18:23 – 19:12; Psalm 146:1 – 10; Proverbs 18:2 – 3
180	June 29	2 Kings 15:1 – 16:20; Acts 19:13 – 41; Psalm 147:1 – 20; Proverbs 18:4 – 5
181	June 30	2 Kings 17:1 – 18:12; Acts 20:1 – 38; Psalm 148:1 – 14; Proverbs 18:6 – 7
182	July 1	2 Kings 18:13 – 19:37; Acts 21:1 – 17; Psalm 149:1 – 9; Proverbs 18:8

BIBLE READING PLANS

DAY	DATE	SCRIPTURE
183	July 2	2 Kings 20:1 – 22:2; Acts 21:18 – 36; Psalm 150:1 – 6; Proverbs 18:9 – 10
184	July 3	2 Kings 22:3 – 23:30; Acts 21:37 – 22:16; Psalm 1:1 – 6; Proverbs 18:11 – 12
185	July 4	2 Kings 23:31 – 25:30; Acts 22:17 – 23:10; Psalm 2:1 – 12; Proverbs 18:13
186	July 5	1 Chronicles 1:1 – 2:17; Acts 23:11 – 35; Psalm 3:1 – 8; Proverbs 18:14 – 15
187	July 6	1 Chronicles 2:18 – 4:4; Acts 24:1 – 27; Psalm 4:1 – 8; Proverbs 18:16 – 18
188	July 7	1 Chronicles 4:5 – 5:17; Acts 25:1 – 27; Psalm 5:1 – 12; Proverbs 18:19
189	July 8	1 Chronicles 5:18 – 6:81; Acts 26:1 – 32; Psalm 6:1 – 10; Proverbs 18:20 – 21
190	July 9	1 Chronicles 7:1 – 8:40; Acts 27:1 – 20; Psalm 7:1 – 17; Proverbs 18:22
191	July 10	1 Chronicles 9:1 – 10:14; Acts 27:21 – 44; Psalm 8:1 – 9; Proverbs 18:23 – 24
192	July 11	1 Chronicles 11:1 – 12:18; Acts 28:1 – 31; Psalm 9:1 – 12; Proverbs 19:1 – 3
193	July 12	1 Chronicles 12:19 – 14:17; Romans 1:1 – 17; Psalm 9:13 – 20; Proverbs 19:4 – 5
194	July 13	1 Chronicles 15:1 – 16:36; Romans 1:18 – 32; Psalm 10:1 – 15; Proverbs 19:6 – 7
195	July 14	1 Chronicles 16:37 – 18:17; Romans 2:1 – 24; Psalm 10:16 – 18; Proverbs 19:8 – 9
196	July 15	1 Chronicles 19:1 – 21:30; Romans 2:25 – 3:8; Psalm 11:1 – 7; Proverbs 19:10 – 12
197	July 16	1 Chronicles 22:1 – 23:32; Romans 3:9 – 31; Psalm 12:1 – 8; Proverbs 19:13 – 14
198	July 17	1 Chronicles 24:1 – 26:11; Romans 4:1 – 12; Psalm 13:1 – 6; Proverbs 19:15 – 16

THE DAILY AUDIO BIBLE READING PLAN

DAY	DATE	SCRIPTURE
199	July 18	1 Chronicles 26:12–27:34; Romans 4:13–5:5; Psalm 14:1–7; Proverbs 19:17
200	July 19	1 Chronicles 28:1–29:30; Romans 5:6–21; Psalm 15:1–5; Proverbs 19:18–19
201	July 20	2 Chronicles 1:1–3:17; Romans 6:1–23; Psalm 16:1–11; Proverbs 19:20–21
202	July 21	2 Chronicles 4:1–6:11; Romans 7:1–13; Psalm 17:1–15; Proverbs 19:22–23
203	July 22	2 Chronicles 6:12–8:10; Romans 7:14–8:8; Psalm 18:1–15; Proverbs 19:24–25
204	July 23	2 Chronicles 8:11–10:19; Romans 8:9–25; Psalm 18:16–36; Proverbs 19:26
205	July 24	2 Chronicles 11:1–13:22; Romans 8:26–39; Psalm 18:37–50; Proverbs 19:27–29
206	July 25	2 Chronicles 14:1–16:14; Romans 9:1–24; Psalm 19:1–14; Proverbs 20:1
207	July 26	2 Chronicles 17:1–18:34; Romans 9:25–10:13; Psalm 20:1–9; Proverbs 20:2–3
208	July 27	2 Chronicles 19:1–20:37; Romans 10:14–11:12; Psalm 21:1–13; Proverbs 20:4–6
209	July 28	2 Chronicles 21:1–23:21; Romans 11:13–36; Psalm 22:1–18; Proverbs 20:7
210	July 29	2 Chronicles 24:1–25:28; Romans 12:1–21; Psalm 22:19–31; Proverbs 20:8–10
211	July 30	2 Chronicles 26:1–28:27; Romans 13:1–14; Psalm 23:1–6; Proverbs 20:11
212	July 31	2 Chronicles 29:1–36; Romans 14:1–23; Psalm 24:1–10; Proverbs 20:12
213	August 1	2 Chronicles 30:1–31:21; Romans 15:1–22; Psalm 25:1–15; Proverbs 20:13–15

BIBLE READING PLANS

DAY	DATE	SCRIPTURE
214	August 2	2 Chronicles 32:1–33:13; Romans 15:23–16:9; Psalm 25:16–22; Proverbs 20:16–18
215	August 3	2 Chronicles 33:14–34:33; Romans 16:10–27; Psalm 26:1–12; Proverbs 20:19
216	August 4	2 Chronicles 35:1–36:23; 1 Corinthians 1:1–17; Psalm 27:1–6; Proverbs 20:20–21
217	August 5	Ezra 1:1–2:70; 1 Corinthians 1:18–2:5; Psalm 27:7–14; Proverbs 20:22–23
218	August 6	Ezra 3:1–4:23; 1 Corinthians 2:6–3:4; Psalm 28:1–9; Proverbs 20:24–25
219	August 7	Ezra 4:24–6:22; 1 Corinthians 3:5–23; Psalm 29:1–11; Proverbs 20:26–27
220	August 8	Ezra 7:1–8:20; 1 Corinthians 4:1–21; Psalm 30:1–12; Proverbs 20:28–30
221	August 9	Ezra 8:21–9:15; 1 Corinthians 5:1–13; Psalm 31:1–8; Proverbs 21:1–2
222	August 10	Ezra 10:1–44; 1 Corinthians 6:1–20; Psalm 31:9–18; Proverbs 21:3
223	August 11	Nehemiah 1:1–3:14; 1 Corinthians 7:1–24; Psalm 31:19–24; Proverbs 21:4
224	August 12	Nehemiah 3:15–5:13; 1 Corinthians 7:25–40; Psalm 32:1–11; Proverbs 21:5–7
225	August 13	Nehemiah 5:14–7:73a; 1 Corinthians 8:1–13; Psalm 33:1–11; Proverbs 21:8–10
226	August 14	Nehemiah 7:73b–9:21; 1 Corinthians 9:1–18; Psalm 33:12–22; Proverbs 21:11–12
227	August 15	Nehemiah 9:22–10:39; 1 Corinthians 9:19–10:13; Psalm 34:1–10; Proverbs 21:13
228	August 16	Nehemiah 11:1–12:26; 1 Corinthians 10:14–33; Psalm 34:11–22; Proverbs 21:14–16

THE DAILY AUDIO BIBLE READING PLAN

DAY	DATE	SCRIPTURE
229	**August 17**	Nehemiah 12:27–13:31; 1 Corinthians 11:1–16; Psalm 35:1–16; Proverbs 21:17–18
230	**August 18**	Esther 1:1–3:15; 1 Corinthians 11:17–34; Psalm 35:17–28; Proverbs 21:19–20
231	**August 19**	Esther 4:1–7:10; 1 Corinthians 12:1–26; Psalm 36:1–12; Proverbs 21:21–22
232	**August 20**	Esther 8:1–10:3; 1 Corinthians 12:27–13:13; Psalm 37:1–11; Proverbs 21:23–24
233	**August 21**	Job 1:1–3:26; 1 Corinthians 14:1–17; Psalm 37:12–29; Proverbs 21:25–26
234	**August 22**	Job 4:1–7:21; 1 Corinthians 14:18–40; Psalm 37:30–40; Proverbs 21:27
235	**August 23**	Job 8:1–11:20; 1 Corinthians 15:1–28; Psalm 38:1–22; Proverbs 21:28–29
236	**August 24**	Job 12:1–15:35; 1 Corinthians 15:29–58; Psalm 39:1–13; Proverbs 21:30–31
237	**August 25**	Job 16:1–19:29; 1 Corinthians 16:1–24; Psalm 40:1–10; Proverbs 22:1
238	**August 26**	Job 20:1–22:30; 2 Corinthians 1:1–11; Psalm 40:11–17; Proverbs 22:2–4
239	**August 27**	Job 23:1–27:23; 2 Corinthians 1:12–2:11; Psalm 41:1–13; Proverbs 22:5–6
240	**August 28**	Job 28:1–30:31; 2 Corinthians 2:12–17; Psalm 42:1–11; Proverbs 22:7
241	**August 29**	Job 31:1–33:33; 2 Corinthians 3:1–18; Psalm 43:1–5; Proverbs 22:8–9
242	**August 30**	Job 34:1–36:33; 2 Corinthians 4:1–12; Psalm 44:1–8; Proverbs 22:10–12
243	**August 31**	Job 37:1–39:30; 2 Corinthians 4:13–5:10; Psalm 44:9–26; Proverbs 22:13
244	**September 1**	Job 40:1–42:17; 2 Corinthians 5:11–21; Psalm 45:1–17; Proverbs 22:14

BIBLE READING PLANS

DAY	DATE	SCRIPTURE
245	**September 2**	Ecclesiastes 1:1 – 3:22; 2 Corinthians 6:1 – 13; Psalm 46:1 – 11; Proverbs 22:15
246	**September 3**	Ecclesiastes 4:1 – 6:12; 2 Corinthians 6:14 – 7:7; Psalm 47:1 – 9; Proverbs 22:16
247	**September 4**	Ecclesiastes 7:1 – 9:18; 2 Corinthians 7:8 – 16; Psalm 48:1 – 14; Proverbs 22:17 – 19
248	**September 5**	Ecclesiastes 10:1 – 12:14; 2 Corinthians 8:1 – 15; Psalm 49:1 – 20; Proverbs 22:20 – 21
249	**September 6**	Song of Songs 1:1 – 4:16; 2 Corinthians 8:16 – 24; Psalm 50:1 – 23; Proverbs 22:22 – 23
250	**September 7**	Song of Songs 5:1 – 8:14; 2 Corinthians 9:1 – 15; Psalm 51:1 – 19; Proverbs 22:24 – 25
251	**September 8**	Isaiah 1:1 – 2:22; 2 Corinthians 10:1 – 18; Psalm 52:1 – 9; Proverbs 22:26 – 27
252	**September 9**	Isaiah 3:1 – 5:30; 2 Corinthians 11:1 – 15; Psalm 53:1 – 6; Proverbs 22:28 – 29
253	**September 10**	Isaiah 6:1 – 7:25; 2 Corinthians 11:16 – 33; Psalm 54:1 – 7; Proverbs 23:1 – 3
254	**September 11**	Isaiah 8:1 – 9:21; 2 Corinthians 12:1 – 10; Psalm 55:1 – 23; Proverbs 23:4 – 5
255	**September 12**	Isaiah 10:1 – 11:16; 2 Corinthians 12:11 – 21; Psalm 56:1 – 13; Proverbs 23:6 – 8
256	**September 13**	Isaiah 12:1 – 14:32; 2 Corinthians 13:1 – 14; Psalm 57:1 – 11; Proverbs 23:9 – 11
257	**September 14**	Isaiah 15:1 – 18:7; Galatians 1:1 – 24; Psalm 58:1 – 11; Proverbs 23:12
258	**September 15**	Isaiah 19:1 – 21:17; Galatians 2:1 – 16; Psalm 59:1 – 17; Proverbs 23:13 – 14
259	**September 16**	Isaiah 22:1 – 24:23; Galatians 2:17 – 3:9; Psalm 60:1 – 12; Proverbs 23:15 – 16
260	**September 17**	Isaiah 25:1 – 28:13; Galatians 3:10 – 22; Psalm 61:1 – 8; Proverbs 23:17 – 18

THE DAILY AUDIO BIBLE READING PLAN

DAY	DATE	SCRIPTURE
261	September 18	Isaiah 28:14–30:11; Galatians 3:23–4:31; Psalm 62:1–12; Proverbs 23:19–21
262	September 19	Isaiah 30:12–33:9; Galatians 5:1–12; Psalm 63:1–11; Proverbs 23:22
263	September 20	Isaiah 33:10–36:22; Galatians 5:13–26; Psalm 64:1–10; Proverbs 23:23
264	September 21	Isaiah 37:1–38:22; Galatians 6:1–18; Psalm 65:1–13; Proverbs 23:24
265	September 22	Isaiah 39:1–41:16; Ephesians 1:1–23; Psalm 66:1–20; Proverbs 23:25–28
266	September 23	Isaiah 41:17–43:13; Ephesians 2:1–22; Psalm 67:1–7; Proverbs 23:29–35
267	September 24	Isaiah 43:14–45:10; Ephesians 3:1–21; Psalm 68:1–18; Proverbs 24:1–2
268	September 25	Isaiah 45:11–48:11; Ephesians 4:1–16; Psalm 68:19–35; Proverbs 24:3–4
269	September 26	Isaiah 48:12–50:11; Ephesians 4:17–32; Psalm 69:1–18; Proverbs 24:5–6
270	September 27	Isaiah 51:1–53:12; Ephesians 5:1–33; Psalm 69:19–36; Proverbs 24:7
271	September 28	Isaiah 54:1–57:13; Ephesians 6:1–24; Psalm 70:1–5; Proverbs 24:8
272	September 29	Isaiah 57:14–59:21; Philippians 1:1–26; Psalm 71:1–24; Proverbs 24:9–10
273	September 30	Isaiah 60:1–62:5; Philippians 1:27–2:18; Psalm 72:1–20; Proverbs 24:11–12
274	October 1	Isaiah 62:6–65:25; Philippians 2:19–30; Psalm 73:1–28; Proverbs 24:13–14
275	October 2	Isaiah 66:1–24; Philippians 3:1–21; Psalm 74:1–23; Proverbs 24:15–16
276	October 3	Jeremiah 1:1–2:30; Philippians 4:1–23; Psalm 75:1–10; Proverbs 24:17–20

BIBLE READING PLANS

DAY	DATE	SCRIPTURE
277	October 4	Jeremiah 2:31 – 4:18; Colossians 1:1 – 17; Psalm 76:1 – 12; Proverbs 24:21 – 22
278	October 5	Jeremiah 4:19 – 6:15; Colossians 1:18 – 2:7; Psalm 77:1 – 20; Proverbs 24:23 – 25
279	October 6	Jeremiah 6:16 – 8:7; Colossians 2:8 – 23; Psalm 78:1 – 31; Proverbs 24:26
280	October 7	Jeremiah 8:8 – 9:26; Colossians 3:1 – 17; Psalm 78:32 – 55; Proverbs 24:27
281	October 8	Jeremiah 10:1 – 11:23; Colossians 3:18 – 4:18; Psalm 78:56 – 72; Proverbs 24:28 – 29
282	October 9	Jeremiah 12:1 – 14:10; 1 Thessalonians 1:1 – 2:12; Psalm 79:1 – 13; Proverbs 24:30 – 34
283	October 10	Jeremiah 14:11 – 16:15; 1 Thessalonians 2:13 – 3:13; Psalm 80:1 – 19; Proverbs 25:1 – 5
284	October 11	Jeremiah 16:16 – 18:23; 1 Thessalonians 4:1 – 5:11; Psalm 81:1 – 16; Proverbs 25:6 – 8
285	October 12	Jeremiah 19:1 – 21:14; 1 Thessalonians 5:12 – 28; Psalm 82:1 – 8; Proverbs 25:9 – 10
286	October 13	Jeremiah 22:1 – 23:20; 2 Thessalonians 1:1 – 12; Psalm 83:1 – 18; Proverbs 25:11 – 14
287	October 14	Jeremiah 23:21 – 25:38; 2 Thessalonians 2:1 – 17; Psalm 84:1 – 12; Proverbs 25:15
288	October 15	Jeremiah 26:1 – 27:22; 2 Thessalonians 3:1 – 18; Psalm 85:1 – 13; Proverbs 25:16
289	October 16	Jeremiah 28:1 – 29:32; 1 Timothy 1:1 – 20; Psalm 86:1 – 17; Proverbs 25:17
290	October 17	Jeremiah 30:1 – 31:26; 1 Timothy 2:1 – 15; Psalm 87:1 – 7; Proverbs 25:18 – 19
291	October 18	Jeremiah 31:27 – 32:44; 1 Timothy 3:1 – 16; Psalm 88:1 – 18; Proverbs 25:20 – 22
292	October 19	Jeremiah 33:1 – 34:22; 1 Timothy 4:1 – 16; Psalm 89:1 – 13; Proverbs 25:23 – 24

THE DAILY AUDIO BIBLE READING PLAN

DAY	DATE	SCRIPTURE
293	October 20	Jeremiah 35:1–36:32; 1 Timothy 5:1–25; Psalm 89:14–37; Proverbs 25:25–27
294	October 21	Jeremiah 37:1–38:28; 1 Timothy 6:1–21; Psalm 89:38–52; Proverbs 25:28
295	October 22	Jeremiah 39:1–41:18; 2 Timothy 1:1–18; Psalm 90:1–91:16; Proverbs 26:1–2
296	October 23	Jeremiah 42:1–44:23; 2 Timothy 2:1–26; Psalm 92:1–93:5; Proverbs 26:3–5
297	October 24	Jeremiah 44:24–47:7; 2 Timothy 3:1–17; Psalm 94:1–23; Proverbs 26:6–8
298	October 25	Jeremiah 48:1–49:22; 2 Timothy 4:1–22; Psalm 95:1–96:13; Proverbs 26:9–12
299	October 26	Jeremiah 49:23–50:46; Titus1:1–16; Psalm 97:1–98:9; Proverbs 26:13–16
300	October 27	Jeremiah 51:1–53; Titus 2:1–15; Psalm 99:1–9; Proverbs 26:17
301	October 28	Jeremiah 51:54–52:34; Titus 3:1–15; Psalm 100:1–5; Proverbs 26:18–19
302	October 29	Lamentations 1:1–2:22; Philemon 1–25; Psalm 101:1–8; Proverbs 26:20
303	October 30	Lamentations 3:1–66; Hebrews 1:1–14; Psalm 102:1–28; Proverbs 26:21–22
304	October 31	Lamentations 4:1–5:22; Hebrews 2:1–18; Psalm 103:1–22; Proverbs 26:23
305	November 1	Ezekiel 1:1–3:15; Hebrews 3:1–19; Psalm 104:1–23; Proverbs 26:24–26
306	November 2	Ezekiel 3:16–6:14; Hebrews 4:1–16; Psalm 104:24–35; Proverbs 26:27
307	November 3	Ezekiel 7:1–9:11; Hebrews 5:1–14; Psalm 105:1–15; Proverbs 26:28
308	November 4	Ezekiel 10:1–11:25; Hebrews 6:1–20; Psalm 105:16–36; Proverbs 27:1–2

BIBLE READING PLANS

DAY	DATE	SCRIPTURE
309	**November 5**	Ezekiel 12:1 – 14:11; Hebrews 7:1 – 17; Psalm 105:37 – 45; Proverbs 27:3
310	**November 6**	Ezekiel 14:12 – 16:41; Hebrews 7:18 – 28; Psalm 106:1 – 12; Proverbs 27:4 – 6
311	**November 7**	Ezekiel 16:42 – 17:24; Hebrews 8:1 – 13; Psalm 106:13 – 31; Proverbs 27:7 – 9
312	**November 8**	Ezekiel 18:1 – 19:14; Hebrews 9:1 – 10; Psalm 106:32 – 48; Proverbs 27:10
313	**November 9**	Ezekiel 20:1 – 49; Hebrews 9:11 – 28; Psalm 107:1 – 43; Proverbs 27:11
314	**November 10**	Ezekiel 21:1 – 22:31; Hebrews 10:1 – 17; Psalm 108:1 – 13; Proverbs 27:12
315	**November 11**	Ezekiel 23:1 – 49; Hebrews 10:18 – 39; Psalm 109:1 – 31; Proverbs 27:13
316	**November 12**	Ezekiel 24:1 – 26:21; Hebrews 11:1 – 16; Psalm 110:1 – 7; Proverbs 27:14
317	**November 13**	Ezekiel 27:1 – 28:26; Hebrews 11:17 – 31; Psalm 111:1 – 10; Proverbs 27:15 – 16
318	**November 14**	Ezekiel 29:1 – 30:26; Hebrews 11:32 – 12:13; Psalm 112:1 – 10; Proverbs 27:17
319	**November 15**	Ezekiel 31:1 – 32:32; Hebrews 12:14 – 29; Psalm 113:1 – 114:8; Proverbs 27:18 – 20
320	**November 16**	Ezekiel 33:1 – 34:31; Hebrews 13:1 – 25; Psalm 115:1 – 18; Proverbs 27:21 – 22
321	**November 17**	Ezekiel 35:1 – 36:38; James 1:1 – 18; Psalm 116:1 – 19; Proverbs 27:23 – 27
322	**November 18**	Ezekiel 37:1 – 38:23; James 1:19 – 2:17; Psalm 117:1 – 2; Proverbs 28:1
323	**November 19**	Ezekiel 39:1 – 40:27; James 2:18 – 3:18; Psalm 118:1 – 18; Proverbs 28:2
324	**November 20**	Ezekiel 40:28 – 41:26; James 4:1 – 17; Psalm 118:19 – 29; Proverbs 28:3 – 5

THE DAILY AUDIO BIBLE READING PLAN

DAY	DATE	SCRIPTURE
325	November 21	Ezekiel 42:1 – 43:27; James 5:1 – 20; Psalm 119:1 – 16; Proverbs 28:6 – 7
326	November 22	Ezekiel 44:1 – 45:12; 1 Peter 1:1 – 12; Psalm 119:17 – 32; Proverbs 28:8 – 10
327	November 23	Ezekiel 45:13 – 46:24; 1 Peter 1:13 – 2:10; Psalm 119:33 – 48; Proverbs 28:11
328	November 24	Ezekiel 47:1 – 48:35; 1 Peter 2:11 – 3:7; Psalm 119:49 – 64; Proverbs 28:12 – 13
329	November 25	Daniel 1:1 – 2:23; 1 Peter 3:8 – 4:6; Psalm 119:65 – 80; Proverbs 28:14
330	November 26	Daniel 2:24 – 3:30; 1 Peter 4:7 – 5:14; Psalm 119:81 – 96; Proverbs 28:15 – 16
331	November 27	Daniel 4:1 – 37; 2 Peter 1:1 – 21; Psalm 119:97 – 112; Proverbs 28:17 – 18
332	November 28	Daniel 5:1 – 31; 2 Peter 2:1 – 22; Psalm 119:113 – 128; Proverbs 28:19 – 20
333	November 29	Daniel 6:1 – 28; 2 Peter 3:1 – 18; Psalm 119:129 – 152; Proverbs 28:21 – 22
334	November 30	Daniel 7:1 – 28; 1 John 1:1 – 10; Psalm 119:153 – 176; Proverbs 28:23 – 24
335	December 1	Daniel 8:1 – 27; 1 John 2:1 – 17; Psalm 120:1 – 7; Proverbs 28:25 – 26
336	December 2	Daniel 9:1 – 11:1; 1 John 2:18 – 3:6; Psalm 121:1 – 8; Proverbs 28:27 – 28
337	December 3	Daniel 11:2 – 35; 1 John 3:7 – 24; Psalm 122:1 – 9; Proverbs 29:1
338	December 4	Daniel 11:36 – 12:13; 1 John 4:1 – 21; Psalm 123:1 – 4; Proverbs 29:2 – 4
339	December 5	Hosea 1:1 – 3:5; 1 John 5:1 – 21; Psalm 124:1 – 8; Proverbs 29:5 – 8
340	December 6	Hosea 4:1 – 5:15; 2 John 1 – 13; Psalm 125:1 – 5; Proverbs 29:9 – 11

BIBLE READING PLANS

DAY	DATE	SCRIPTURE
341	**December 7**	Hosea 6:1 – 9:17; 3 John 1 – 15; Psalm 126:1 – 6; Proverbs 29:12 – 14
342	**December 8**	Hosea 10:1 – 14:9; Jude 1 – 25; Psalm 127:1 – 5; Proverbs 29:15 – 17
343	**December 9**	Joel 1:1 – 3:21; Revelation 1:1 – 20; Psalm 128:1 – 6; Proverbs 29:18
344	**December 10**	Amos 1:1 – 3:15; Revelation 2:1 – 17; Psalm 129:1 – 8; Proverbs 29:19 – 20
345	**December 11**	Amos 4:1 – 6:14; Revelation 2:18 – 3:6; Psalm 130:1 – 8; Proverbs 29:21 – 22
346	**December 12**	Amos 7:1 – 9:15; Revelation 3:7 – 22; Psalm 131:1 – 3; Proverbs 29:23
347	**December 13**	Obadiah 1 – 21; Revelation 4:1 – 11; Psalm 132:1 – 18; Proverbs 29:24 – 25
348	**December 14**	Jonah 1:1 – 4:11; Revelation 5:1 – 14; Psalm 133:1 – 3; Proverbs 29:26 – 27
349	**December 15**	Micah 1:1 – 4:13; Revelation 6:1 – 17; Psalm 134:1 – 3; Proverbs 30:1 – 4
350	**December 16**	Micah 5:1 – 7:20; Revelation 7:1 – 17; Psalm 135:1 – 21; Proverbs 30:5 – 6
351	**December 17**	Nahum 1:1 – 3:19; Revelation 8:1 – 13; Psalm 136:1 – 26; Proverbs 30:7 – 9
352	**December 18**	Habakkuk 1:1 – 3:19; Revelation 9:1 – 21; Psalm 137:1 – 9; Proverbs 30:10
353	**December 19**	Zephaniah 1:1 – 3:20; Revelation 10:1 – 11; Psalm 138:1 – 8; Proverbs 30:11 – 14
354	**December 20**	Haggai 1:1 – 2:23; Revelation 11:1 – 19; Psalm 139:1 – 24; Proverbs 30:15 – 16
355	**December 21**	Zechariah 1:1 – 21; Revelation 12:1 – 17; Psalm 140:1 – 13; Proverbs 30:17
356	**December 22**	Zechariah 2:1 – 3:10; Revelation 13:1 – 18; Psalm 141:1 – 10; Proverbs 30:18 – 20

THE DAILY AUDIO BIBLE READING PLAN

DAY	DATE	SCRIPTURE
357	December 23	Zechariah 4:1 – 5:11; Revelation 14:1 – 20; Psalm 142:1 – 7; Proverbs 30:21 – 23
358	December 24	Zechariah 6:1 – 7:14; Revelation 15:1 – 8; Psalm 143:1 – 12; Proverbs 30:24 – 28
359	December 25	Zechariah 8:1 – 23; Revelation 16:1 – 21; Psalm 144:1 – 15; Proverbs 30:29 – 31
360	December 26	Zechariah 9:1 – 17; Revelation 17:1 – 18; Psalm 145:1 – 21; Proverbs 30:32
361	December 27	Zechariah 10:1 – 11:17; Revelation 18:1 – 24; Psalm 146:1 – 10; Proverbs 30:33
362	December 28	Zechariah 12:1 – 13:9; Revelation 19:1 – 21; Psalm 147:1 – 20; Proverbs 31:1 – 7
363	December 29	Zechariah 14:1 – 21; Revelation 20:1 – 15; Psalm 148:1 – 14; Proverbs 31:8 – 9
364	December 30	Malachi 1:1 – 2:17; Revelation 21:1 – 27; Psalm 149:1 – 9; Proverbs 31:10 – 24
365	December 31	Malachi 3:1 – 4:6; Revelation 22:1 – 21; Psalm 150:1 – 6; Proverbs 31:25 – 31

The Chronological Bible in a Year

Reading the Bible chronologically allows you to follow the timeline of how events occurred. It gives you a "real time" outlook on how things unfolded in history. For example, it is strongly believed that the story of Job is one of the earliest stories of inspired Scripture and pre-dates Abraham and the covenantal relationship he had with God. Therefore the story of Job interrupts the book of Genesis in order to fall into its place chronologically. If you like to think linear and desire to read the Bible literally "front to back," this may be a good choice for you.

DAY	DATE	SCRIPTURE
1	January 1	Genesis 1–3
2	January 2	Genesis 4–7
3	January 3	Genesis 8–11
4	January 4	Job 1–5
5	January 5	Job 6–7
6	January 6	Job 10–13
7	January 7	Job 14–16
8	January 8	Job 17–20
9	January 9	Job 21–23
10	January 10	Job 24–28
11	January 11	Job 29–31
12	January 12	Job 32–34
13	January 13	Job 35–37

THE CHRONOLOGICAL BIBLE IN A YEAR

DAY	DATE	SCRIPTURE
14	January 14	Job 38–39
15	January 15	Job 40–42
16	January 16	Genesis 12–15
17	January 17	Genesis 16–18
18	January 18	Genesis 19–21
19	January 19	Genesis 22–24
20	January 20	Genesis 25–26
21	January 21	Genesis 27–29
22	January 22	Genesis 30–31
23	January 23	Genesis 32–34
24	January 24	Genesis 35–37
25	January 25	Genesis 38–40
26	January 26	Genesis 41–42
27	January 27	Genesis 43–45
28	January 28	Genesis 46–47
29	January 29	Genesis 48–50
30	January 30	Exodus 1–3
31	January 31	Exodus 4–6
32	February 1	Exodus 7–9
33	February 2	Exodus 10–12
34	February 3	Exodus 13–15
35	February 4	Exodus 16–18
36	February 5	Exodus 19–21

BIBLE READING PLANS

DAY	DATE	SCRIPTURE
37	February 6	Exodus 22–24
38	February 7	Exodus 25–27
39	February 8	Exodus 28–29
40	February 9	Exodus 30–32
41	February 10	Exodus 33–35
42	February 11	Exodus 36–38
43	February 12	Exodus 39–40
44	February 13	Leviticus 1–4
45	February 14	Leviticus 5–7
46	February 15	Leviticus 8–10
47	February 16	Leviticus 11–13
48	February 17	Leviticus 14–15
49	February 18	Leviticus 16–18
50	February 19	Leviticus 19–21
51	February 20	Leviticus 22–23
52	February 21	Leviticus 24–25
53	February 22	Leviticus 26–27
54	February 23	Numbers 1–2
55	February 24	Numbers 3–4
56	February 25	Numbers 5–6
57	February 26	Numbers 7
58	February 27	Numbers 8–10
59	February 28	Numbers 11–13

THE CHRONOLOGICAL BIBLE IN A YEAR

DAY	DATE	SCRIPTURE
60	March 1	Numbers 14–15; Psalm 90
61	March 2	Numbers 16–17
62	March 3	Numbers 18–20
63	March 4	Numbers 21–22
64	March 5	Numbers 23–25
65	March 6	Numbers 26–27
66	March 7	Numbers 28–30
67	March 8	Numbers 31–32
68	March 9	Numbers 33–34
69	March 10	Numbers 35–36
70	March 11	Deuteronomy 1–2
71	March 12	Deuteronomy 3–4
72	March 13	Deuteronomy 5–7
73	March 14	Deuteronomy 8–10
74	March 15	Deuteronomy 11–13
75	March 16	Deuteronomy 14–16
76	March 17	Deuteronomy 17–20
77	March 18	Deuteronomy 21–23
78	March 19	Deuteronomy 24–27
79	March 20	Deuteronomy 28–29
80	March 21	Deuteronomy 30–31
81	March 22	Deuteronomy 32–34; Psalm 91
82	March 23	Joshua 1–4

BIBLE READING PLANS

DAY	DATE	SCRIPTURE
83	March 24	Joshua 5–8
84	March 25	Joshua 9–11
85	March 26	Joshua 12–15
86	March 27	Joshua 16–18
87	March 28	Joshua 19–21
88	March 29	Joshua 22–24
89	March 30	Judges 1–2
90	March 31	Judges 3–5
91	April 1	Judges 6–7
92	April 2	Judges 8–9
93	April 3	Judges 10–12
94	April 4	Judges 13–15
95	April 5	Judges 16–18
96	April 6	Judges 19–21
97	April 7	Ruth
98	April 8	1 Samuel 1–3
99	April 9	1 Samuel 4–8
100	April 10	1 Samuel 9–12
101	April 11	1 Samuel 13–14
102	April 12	1 Samuel 15–17
103	April 13	1 Samuel 18–20; Psalms 11/59
104	April 14	1 Samuel 21–24
105	April 15	Psalms 7/27/31/34/52

THE CHRONOLOGICAL BIBLE IN A YEAR

DAY	DATE	SCRIPTURE
106	April 16	Psalms 56/120/140–142
107	April 17	1 Samuel 25–27
108	April 18	Psalms 17/35/54/63
109	April 19	1 Samuel 28–31; Psalm 18
110	April 20	Psalms 121/123–125/128–130
111	April 21	2 Samuel 1–4
112	April 22	Psalms 6/8–10/14/16/19/21
113	April 23	1 Chronicles 1–2
114	April 24	Psalms 43–45/49/84–85/87
115	April 25	1 Chronicles 3–5
116	April 26	Psalms 73/77–78
117	April 27	1 Chronicles 6
118	April 28	Psalms 81/88/92–93
119	April 29	1 Chronicles 7–10
120	April 30	Psalms 102–104
121	May 1	2 Samuel 5:1–10; 1 Chronicles 11–12
122	May 2	Psalm 133
123	May 3	Psalms 106–107
124	May 4	2 Samuel 5:11–6:23; 1 Chronicles 13–16
125	May 5	Psalms 1–2/15/22–24/47/68
126	May 6	Psalms 89/96/100–101/105/132
127	May 7	2 Samuel 7; 1 Chronicles 17
128	May 8	Psalms 25/29/33/36/39

BIBLE READING PLANS

DAY	DATE	SCRIPTURE
129	May 9	2 Samuel 8–9; 1 Chronicles 18
130	May 10	Psalms 50/53/60/75
131	May 11	2 Samuel 10; 1 Chronicles 19; Psalm 20
132	May 12	Psalms 65–67/69–70
133	May 13	2 Samuel 11–12; 1 Chronicles 20
134	May 14	Psalms 32/51/86/122
135	May 15	2 Samuel 13–15
136	May 16	Psalms 3–4/12–13/28/55
137	May 17	2 Samuel 16–18
138	May 18	Psalms 26/40/58/61–62/64
139	May 19	2 Samuel 19–21
140	May 20	Psalms 5/38/41–42
141	May 21	2 Samuel 22–23; Psalm 57
142	May 22	Psalms 95/97–99
143	May 23	2 Samuel 24; 1 Chronicles 21–22; Psalm 30
144	May 24	Psalms 108–110
145	May 25	1 Chronicles 23–25
146	May 26	Psalms 131/138–139/143–145
147	May 27	1 Chronicles 26–29; Psalms 127
148	May 28	Psalms 111–118
149	May 29	1 Kings 1–2; Psalms 37/71/94
150	May 30	Psalm 119:1–88
151	May 31	1 Kings 3–4; 2 Chronicles 1; Psalm 72

THE CHRONOLOGICAL BIBLE IN A YEAR

DAY	DATE	· SCRIPTURE
152	June 1	Psalm 119:89 – 176
153	June 2	Song of Songs
154	June 3	Proverbs 1 – 3
155	June 4	Proverbs 4 – 6
156	June 5	Proverbs 7 – 9
157	June 6	Proverbs 10 – 12
158	June 7	Proverbs 13 – 15
159	June 8	Proverbs 16 – 18
160	June 9	Proverbs 19 – 21
161	June 10	Proverbs 22 – 24
162	June 11	1 Kings 5 – 6; 2 Chronicles 2 – 3
163	June 12	1 Kings 7; 2 Chronicles 4
164	June 13	1 Kings 8; 2 Chronicles 5
165	June 14	2 Chronicles 6 – 7; Psalm 136
166	June 15	Psalms 134/146 – 150
167	June 16	1 Kings 9; 2 Chronicles 8
168	June 17	Proverbs 25 – 26
169	June 18	Proverbs 27 – 29
170	June 19	Ecclesiastes 1 – 6
171	June 20	Ecclesiastes 7 – 12
172	June 21	1 Kings 10 – 11; 2 Chronicles 9
173	June 22	Proverbs 30 – 31
174	June 23	1 Kings 12 – 14

BIBLE READING PLANS

DAY	DATE	SCRIPTURE
175	June 24	2 Chronicles 10–12
176	June 25	1 Kings 15:1–24; 2 Chronicles 13–16
177	June 26	1 Kings 15:25–16:34; 2 Chronicles 17
178	June 27	1 Kings 17–19
179	June 28	1 Kings 20–21
180	June 29	1 Kings 22; 2 Chronicles 18
181	June 30	2 Chronicles 19–23
182	July 1	Obadiah; Psalms 82–83
183	July 2	2 Kings 1–4
184	July 3	2 Kings 5–8
185	July 4	2 Kings 9–11
186	July 5	2 Kings 12–13; 2 Chronicles 24
187	July 6	2 Kings 14; 2 Chronicles 25
188	July 7	Jonah
189	July 8	2 Kings 15; 2 Chronicles 26
190	July 9	Isaiah 1–4
191	July 10	Isaiah 5–8
192	July 11	Amos 1–5
193	July 12	Amos 6–9
194	July 13	2 Chronicles 27; Isaiah 9–12
195	July 14	Micah
196	July 15	2 Chronicles 28; 2 Kings 16–17
197	July 16	Isaiah 13–17

THE CHRONOLOGICAL BIBLE IN A YEAR

DAY	DATE	SCRIPTURE
198	July 17	Isaiah 18–22
199	July 18	Isaiah 23–27
200	July 19	2 Kings 18:1–8; 2 Chronicles 29–31; Psalm 48
201	July 20	Hosea 1–7
202	July 21	Hosea 8–14
203	July 22	Isaiah 28–30
204	July 23	Isaiah 31–34
205	July 24	Isaiah 35–36
206	July 25	Isaiah 37–39; Psalm 76
207	July 26	Isaiah 40–43
208	July 27	Isaiah 44–48
209	July 28	2 Kings 18:9–19:37; Psalms 46/80/135
210	July 29	Isaiah 49–53
211	July 30	Isaiah 54–58
212	July 31	Isaiah 59–63
213	August 1	Isaiah 64–66
214	August 2	2 Kings 20–21
215	August 3	2 Chronicles 32–33
216	August 4	Nahum
217	August 5	2 Kings 22–23; 2 Chronicles 34–35
218	August 6	Zephaniah
219	August 7	Jeremiah 1–3
220	August 8	Jeremiah 4–6

BIBLE READING PLANS

DAY	DATE	SCRIPTURE
221	**August 9**	Jeremiah 7–9
222	**August 10**	Jeremiah 10–13
223	**August 11**	Jeremiah 14–17
224	**August 12**	Jeremiah 18–22
225	**August 13**	Jeremiah 23–25
226	**August 14**	Jeremiah 26–29
227	**August 15**	Jeremiah 30–31
228	**August 16**	Jeremiah 32–34
229	**August 17**	Jeremiah 35–37
230	**August 18**	Jeremiah 38–40; Psalms 74/79
231	**August 19**	2 Kings 24–25; 2 Chronicles 36
232	**August 20**	Habakkuk
233	**August 21**	Jeremiah 41–45
234	**August 22**	Jeremiah 46–48
235	**August 23**	Jeremiah 49–50
236	**August 24**	Jeremiah 51–52
237	**August 25**	Lamentations 1:1–3:36
238	**August 26**	Lamentations 3:37–5:22
239	**August 27**	Ezekiel 1–4
240	**August 28**	Ezekiel 5–8
241	**August 29**	Ezekiel 9–12
242	**August 30**	Ezekiel 13–15
243	**August 31**	Ezekiel 16–17

THE CHRONOLOGICAL BIBLE IN A YEAR

DAY	DATE	SCRIPTURE
244	September 1	Ezekiel 18–19
245	September 2	Ezekiel 20–21
246	September 3	Ezekiel 22–23
247	September 4	Ezekiel 24–27
248	September 5	Ezekiel 28–31
249	September 6	Ezekiel 32–34
250	September 7	Ezekiel 35–37
251	September 8	Ezekiel 38–39
252	September 9	Ezekiel 40–41
253	September 10	Ezekiel 42–43
254	September 11	Ezekiel 44–45
255	September 12	Ezekiel 46–48
256	September 13	Joel
257	September 14	Daniel 1–3
258	September 15	Daniel 4–6
259	September 16	Daniel 7–9
260	September 17	Daniel 10–12
261	September 18	Ezra 1–3
262	September 19	Ezra 4–6; Psalm 137
263	September 20	Haggai
264	September 21	Zechariah 1–7
265	September 22	Zechariah 8–14
266	September 23	Esther 1–5

BIBLE READING PLANS

DAY	DATE	SCRIPTURE
267	September 24	Esther 6–10
268	September 25	Ezra 7–10
269	September 26	Nehemiah 1–5
270	September 27	Nehemiah 6–7
271	September 28	Nehemiah 8–10
272	September 29	Nehemiah 11–13; Psalm 126
273	September 30	Malachi
274	October 1	Luke 1; John 1:1–14
275	October 2	Matthew 1; Luke 2:1–38
276	October 3	Matthew 2; Luke 2:39–52
277	October 4	Matthew 3; Mark 1; Luke 3
278	October 5	Matthew 4; Luke 4–5; John 1:15–51
279	October 6	John 2–4
280	October 7	Mark 2
281	October 8	John 5
282	October 9	Matthew 12:1–21; Mark 3; Luke 6
283	October 10	Matthew 5–7
284	October 11	Matthew 8:1–13; Luke 7
285	October 12	Matthew 11
286	October 13	Matthew 12:22–50
287	October 14	Matthew 13; Luke 8
288	October 15	Matthew 8:14–34; Mark 4–5
289	October 16	Matthew 9–10

DAY	DATE	SCRIPTURE
290	October 17	Matthew 14; Mark 6; Luke 9:1–17
291	October 18	John 6
292	October 19	Matthew 15; Mark 7
293	October 20	Matthew 16; Mark 8; Luke 9:18–27
294	October 21	Matthew 17; Mark 9; Luke 9:28–62
295	October 22	Matthew 18
296	October 23	John 7–8
297	October 24	John 9:1–10:21
298	October 25	Luke 10–11; John 10:22–42
299	October 26	Luke 12–13
300	October 27	Luke 14–15
301	October 28	Luke 16–17:10
302	October 29	John 11
303	October 30	Luke 17:11–18:14
304	October 31	Matthew 19; Mark 10
305	November 1	Matthew 20–21
306	November 2	Luke 18:15–19:48
307	November 3	Mark 11; John 12
308	November 4	Matthew 22; Mark 12
309	November 5	Matthew 23; Luke 20–21
310	November 6	Mark 13
311	November 7	Matthew 24
312	November 8	Matthew 25

BIBLE READING PLANS

DAY	DATE	SCRIPTURE
313	**November 9**	Matthew 26; Mark 14
314	**November 10**	Luke 22; John 13
315	**November 11**	John 14 – 17
316	**November 12**	Matthew 27; Mark 15
317	**November 13**	Luke 23; John 18 – 19
318	**November 14**	Matthew 28; Mark 16
319	**November 15**	Luke 24; John 20 – 21
320	**November 16**	Acts 1 – 3
321	**November 17**	Acts 4 – 6
322	**November 18**	Acts 7 – 8
323	**November 19**	Acts 9 – 10
324	**November 20**	Acts 11 – 12
325	**November 21**	Acts 13 – 14
326	**November 22**	James
327	**November 23**	Acts 15 – 16
328	**November 24**	Galatians 1 – 3
329	**November 25**	Galatians 4 – 6
330	**November 26**	Acts 17 – 18:18
331	**November 27**	1 Thessalonians; 2 Thessalonians
332	**November 28**	Acts 18:19 – 19:41
333	**November 29**	1 Corinthians 1 – 4
334	**November 30**	1 Corinthians 5 – 8
335	**December 1**	1 Corinthians 9 – 11

THE CHRONOLOGICAL BIBLE IN A YEAR

DAY	DATE	SCRIPTURE
336	December 2	1 Corinthians 12–14
337	December 3	1 Corinthians 15–16
338	December 4	2 Corinthians 1–4
339	December 5	2 Corinthians 5–9
340	December 6	2 Corinthians 10–13
341	December 7	Acts 20:1–3; Romans 1–3
342	December 8	Romans 4–7
343	December 9	Romans 8–10
344	December 10	Romans 11–13
345	December 11	Romans 14–16
346	December 12	Acts 20:4–23:35
347	December 13	Acts 24–26
348	December 14	Acts 27–28
349	December 15	Colossians; Philemon
350	December 16	Ephesians
351	December 17	Philippians
352	December 18	1 Timothy
353	December 19	Titus
354	December 20	1 Peter
355	December 21	Hebrews 1–6
356	December 22	Hebrews 7–10
357	December 23	Hebrews 11–13
358	December 24	2 Timothy

BIBLE READING PLANS

DAY	DATE	SCRIPTURE
359	**December 25**	2 Peter; Jude
360	**December 26**	1 John
361	**December 27**	2/3 John
362	**December 28**	Revelation 1–5
363	**December 29**	Revelation 6–11
364	**December 30**	Revelation 12–18
365	**December 31**	Revelation 19–22

The Historical Bible in a Year

Reading through the Bible historically is not the same as reading it chronologically as the name might imply. If you dedicate yourself to reading the Bible historically, you will read it in the order that the books, poems, and letters were inspired. This isn't the same as reading the events as they happened. Many books are prophetic and many speak of things that have already occurred. The historical reading plan uses the best scholarship we currently have to allow you to read the books in the order that they were given to us.

DAY	DATE	SCRIPTURE
1	January 1	Genesis 1–3
2	January 2	Genesis 4–7
3	January 3	Genesis 8–11
4	January 4	Genesis 12–15
5	January 5	Genesis 16–18
6	January 6	Genesis 19–21
7	January 7	Genesis 22–24
8	January 8	Genesis 25–26
9	January 9	Genesis 27–29
10	January 10	Genesis 30–31
11	January 11	Genesis 32–34
12	January 12	Genesis 35–37
13	January 13	Genesis 38–40
14	January 14	Genesis 41–42

BIBLE READING PLANS

DAY	DATE	SCRIPTURE
15	**January 15**	Genesis 43–45
16	**January 16**	Genesis 46–47
17	**January 17**	Genesis 48–50
18	**January 18**	Exodus 1–3
19	**January 19**	Exodus 4:–6
20	**January 20**	Exodus 7–9
21	**January 21**	Exodus 10–12
22	**January 22**	Exodus 13–15
23	**January 23**	Exodus 16–18
24	**January 24**	Exodus 19–21
25	**January 25**	Exodus 22–24
26	**January 26**	Exodus 25–27
27	**January 27**	Exodus 28–29
28	**January 28**	Exodus 30–32
29	**January 29**	Exodus 33–35
30	**January 30**	Exodus 36–38
31	**January 31**	Exodus 39–40
32	**February 1**	Leviticus 1–4
33	**February 2**	Leviticus 5–7
34	**February 3**	Leviticus 8–10
35	**February 4**	Leviticus 11–13
36	**February 5**	Leviticus 14–15
37	**February 6**	Leviticus 16–18

THE HISTORICAL BIBLE IN A YEAR

DAY	DATE	SCRIPTURE
38	**February 7**	Leviticus 19–21
39	**February 8**	Leviticus 22–23
40	**February 9**	Leviticus 24–25
41	**February 10**	Leviticus 26–27
42	**February 11**	Numbers 1–2
43	**February 12**	Numbers 3–4
44	**February 13**	Numbers 5–6
45	**February 14**	Numbers 7
46	**February 15**	Numbers 8–10
47	**February 16**	Numbers 11–13
48	**February 17**	Numbers 14–15
49	**February 18**	Numbers 16–17
50	**February 19**	Numbers 18–20
51	**February 20**	Numbers 21–22
52	**February 21**	Numbers 23–25
53	**February 22**	Numbers 26–27
54	**February 23**	Numbers 28–30
55	**February 24**	Numbers 31–32
56	**February 25**	Numbers 33–34
57	**February 26**	Numbers 35–36
58	**February 27**	Deuteronomy 1–2
59	**February 28**	Deuteronomy 3–4
60	**March 1**	Deuteronomy 5–7

BIBLE READING PLANS

DAY	DATE	SCRIPTURE
61	March 2	Deuteronomy 8–10
62	March 3	Deuteronomy 11–13
63	March 4	Deuteronomy 14–16
64	March 5	Deuteronomy 17–20
65	March 6	Deuteronomy 21–23
66	March 7	Deuteronomy 24–27
67	March 8	Deuteronomy 28–29
68	March 9	Deuteronomy 30–31
69	March 10	Deuteronomy 32–34
70	March 11	Joshua 1–4
71	March 12	Joshua 5–8
72	March 13	Joshua 9–11
73	March 14	Joshua 12–15
74	March 15	Joshua 16–18
75	March 16	Joshua 19–21
76	March 17	Joshua 22–24
77	March 18	Judges 1–2
78	March 19	Judges 3–5
79	March 20	Judges 6–7
80	March 21	Judges 8–9
81	March 22	Judges 10–12
82	March 23	Judges 13–15
83	March 24	Judges 16–18

DAY	DATE	SCRIPTURE
84	**March 25**	Judges 19–21
85	**March 26**	1 Samuel 1–3
86	**March 27**	1 Samuel 4–8
87	**March 28**	1 Samuel 9–12
88	**March 29**	1 Samuel 13–14
89	**March 30**	1 Samuel 15–17
90	**March 31**	1 Samuel 18–20
91	**April 1**	1 Samuel 21–24
92	**April 2**	1 Samuel 25–27
93	**April 3**	1 Samuel 28–31
94	**April 4**	2 Samuel 1–3
95	**April 5**	2 Samuel 4–6
96	**April 6**	2 Samuel 7–10
97	**April 7**	2 Samuel 11–13
98	**April 8**	2 Samuel 14–15
99	**April 9**	2 Samuel 16–18
100	**April 10**	2 Samuel 19–21
101	**April 11**	2 Samuel 22–24
102	**April 12**	1 Kings 1–2
103	**April 13**	1 Kings 3–5
104	**April 14**	1 Kings 6–7
105	**April 15**	1 Kings 8–9
106	**April 16**	1 Kings 10–11

BIBLE READING PLANS

DAY	DATE	SCRIPTURE
107	April 17	1 Kings 12 – 14
108	April 18	1 Kings 15 – 17
109	April 19	1 Kings 18 – 20
110	April 20	1 Kings 21 – 22
111	April 21	2 Kings 1 – 4
112	April 22	2 Kings 5 – 8
113	April 23	2 Kings 9 – 11
114	April 24	2 Kings 12 – 14
115	April 25	2 Kings 15 – 17
116	April 26	2 Kings 18 – 19
117	April 27	2 Kings 20 – 22
118	April 28	2 Kings 23 – 25
119	April 29	Isaiah 1 – 4
120	April 30	Isaiah 5 – 8
121	May 1	Isaiah 9 – 12
122	May 2	Isaiah 13 – 17
123	May 3	Isaiah 18 – 22
124	May 4	Isaiah 23 – 27
125	May 5	Isaiah 28 – 30
126	May 6	Isaiah 31 – 35
127	May 7	Isaiah 36 – 41
128	May 8	Isaiah 42 – 44
129	May 9	Isaiah 45 – 48

THE HISTORICAL BIBLE IN A YEAR

DAY	DATE	SCRIPTURE
130	May 10	Isaiah 49 – 53
131	May 11	Isaiah 54 – 58
132	May 12	Isaiah 59 – 63
133	May 13	Isaiah 64 – 66
134	May 14	Jeremiah 1 – 3
135	May 15	Jeremiah 4 – 6
136	May 16	Jeremiah 7 – 9
137	May 17	Jeremiah 10 – 13
138	May 18	Jeremiah 14 – 17
139	May 19	Jeremiah 18 – 22
140	May 20	Jeremiah 23 – 25
141	May 21	Jeremiah 26 – 29
142	May 22	Jeremiah 30 – 31
143	May 23	Jeremiah 32 – 34
144	May 24	Jeremiah 35 – 37
145	May 25	Jeremiah 38 – 41
146	May 26	Jeremiah 42 – 45
147	May 27	Jeremiah 46 – 48
148	May 28	Jeremiah 49 – 50
149	May 29	Jeremiah 51 – 52
150	May 30	Ezekiel 1 – 3
151	May 31	Ezekiel 4 – 7
152	June 1	Ezekiel 8 – 10

BIBLE READING PLANS

DAY	DATE	SCRIPTURE
153	June 2	Ezekiel 11 – 12
154	June 3	Ezekiel 13 – 15
155	June 4	Ezekiel 16 – 17
156	June 5	Ezekiel 18 – 20
157	June 6	Ezekiel 21 – 23
158	June 7	Ezekiel 24 – 27
159	June 8	Ezekiel 28 – 31
160	June 9	Ezekiel 32 – 34
161	June 10	Ezekiel 35 – 38
162	June 11	Ezekiel 39 – 41
163	June 12	Ezekiel 42 – 43
164	June 13	Ezekiel 44 – 45
165	June 14	Ezekiel 46 – 48
166	June 15	Hosea 1 – 7
167	June 16	Hosea 8 – 14
168	June 17	Joel
169	June 18	Amos 1 – 5
170	June 19	Amos 6 – 9
171	June 20	Obadiah; Jonah
172	June 21	Micah
173	June 22	Nahum; Habakkuk
174	June 23	Zephaniah; Haggai
175	June 24	Zechariah 1 – 7

DAY	DATE	SCRIPTURE
176	June 25	Zechariah 8–14
177	June 26	Malachi
178	June 27	Psalms 1–8
179	June 28	Psalms 9–16
180	June 29	Psalms 17–20
181	June 30	Psalms 21–25
182	July 1	Psalms 26–31
183	July 2	Psalms 32–35
184	July 3	Psalms 36–39
185	July 4	Psalms 40–45
186	July 5	Psalms 46–50
187	July 6	Psalms 51–57
188	July 7	Psalms 58–65
189	July 8	Psalms 66–69
190	July 9	Psalms 70–73
191	July 10	Psalms 74–77
192	July 11	Psalms 78–79
193	July 12	Psalms 80–85
194	July 13	Psalms 86–89
195	July 14	Psalms 90–95
196	July 15	Psalms 96–102
197	July 16	Psalms 103–105
198	July 17	Psalms 106–107

BIBLE READING PLANS

DAY	DATE	SCRIPTURE
199	July 18	Psalms 108–114
200	July 19	Psalms 115–118
201	July 20	Psalm 119:1–88
202	July 21	Psalm 119:89–176
203	July 22	Psalms 120–132
204	July 23	Psalms 133–139
205	July 24	Psalms 140–145
206	July 25	Psalms 146–150
207	July 26	Proverbs 1–3
208	July 27	Proverbs 4–6
209	July 28	Proverbs 7–9
210	July 29	Proverbs 10–12
211	July 30	Proverbs 13–15
212	July 31	Proverbs 16–18
213	August 1	Proverbs 19–21
214	August 2	Proverbs 22–23
215	August 3	Proverbs 24–26
216	August 4	Proverbs 27–29
217	August 5	Proverbs 30–31
218	August 6	Job 1–5
219	August 7	Job 6–9
220	August 8	Job 10–13
221	August 9	Job 14–16

DAY	DATE	SCRIPTURE
222	**August 10**	Job 17–20
223	**August 11**	Job 21–23
224	**August 12**	Job 24–28
225	**August 13**	Job 29–31
226	**August 14**	Job 32–34
227	**August 15**	Job 35–37
228	**August 16**	Job 38–39
229	**August 17**	Job 40–42
230	**August 18**	Song of Songs
231	**August 19**	Ruth
232	**August 20**	Lamentations 1–3:36
233	**August 21**	Lamentations 3:37–5:22
234	**August 22**	Ecclesiastes 1–4
235	**August 23**	Ecclesiastes 5–8
236	**August 24**	Ecclesiastes 9–12
237	**August 25**	Esther 1–3
238	**August 26**	Esther 4–6
239	**August 27**	Esther 7–10
240	**August 28**	Daniel 1–2
241	**August 29**	Daniel 3–4
242	**August 30**	Daniel 5–6
243	**August 31**	Daniel 7–8
244	**September 1**	Daniel 9–10

BIBLE READING PLANS

DAY	DATE	SCRIPTURE
245	September 2	Daniel 11–12
246	September 3	Ezra 1–2
247	September 4	Ezra 3–5
248	September 5	Ezra 6–7
249	September 6	Ezra 8–10
250	September 7	Nehemiah 1–3
251	September 8	Nehemiah 4–6
252	September 9	Nehemiah 7–8
253	September 10	Nehemiah 9–11
254	September 11	Nehemiah 12–13
255	September 12	1 Chronicles 1–2
256	September 13	1 Chronicles 3–5
257	September 14	1 Chronicles 6
258	September 15	1 Chronicles 7–8
259	September 16	1 Chronicles 9–10
260	September 17	1 Chronicles 11–12
261	September 18	1 Chronicles 13–15
262	September 19	1 Chronicles 16–17
263	September 20	1 Chronicles 18–20
264	September 21	1 Chronicles 21–23
265	September 22	1 Chronicles 24–25
266	September 23	1 Chronicles 26–27
267	September 24	1 Chronicles 28–29

DAY	DATE	SCRIPTURE
268	September 25	2 Chronicles 1 – 4
269	September 26	2 Chronicles 5 – 7
270	September 27	2 Chronicles 8 – 10
271	September 28	2 Chronicles 11 – 14
272	September 29	2 Chronicles 15 – 18
273	September 30	2 Chronicles 19 – 21
274	October 1	2 Chronicles 22 – 24
275	October 2	2 Chronicles 25 – 27
276	October 3	2 Chronicles 28 – 29
277	October 4	2 Chronicles 30 – 32
278	October 5	2 Chronicles 33 – 34
279	October 6	2 Chronicles 35 – 36
280	October 7	James
281	October 8	Galatians 1 – 3
282	October 9	Galatians 4 – 6
283	October 10	1 Thessalonians
284	October 11	2 Thessalonians
285	October 12	1 Corinthians 1 – 4
286	October 13	1 Corinthians 5 – 8
287	October 14	1 Corinthians 9 – 11
288	October 15	1 Corinthians 12 – 14
289	October 16	1 Corinthians 15 – 16
290	October 17	2 Corinthians 1 – 4

BIBLE READING PLANS

DAY	DATE	SCRIPTURE
291	**October 18**	2 Corinthians 5 – 9
292	**October 19**	2 Corinthians 10 – 13
293	**October 20**	Romans 1 – 3
294	**October 21**	Romans 4 – 7
295	**October 22**	Romans 8 – 10
296	**October 23**	Romans 11 – 13
297	**October 24**	Romans 14 – 16
298	**October 25**	Matthew 1 – 4
299	**October 26**	Matthew 5 – 7
300	**October 27**	Matthew 8 – 9
301	**October 28**	Matthew 10 – 12
302	**October 29**	Matthew 13 – 14
303	**October 30**	Matthew 15 – 17
304	**October 31**	Matthew 18 – 20
305	**November 1**	Matthew 21 – 22
306	**November 2**	Matthew 23 – 24
307	**November 3**	Matthew 25 – 26
308	**November 4**	Matthew 27 – 28
309	**November 5**	Mark 1 – 3
310	**November 6**	Mark 4 – 5
311	**November 7**	Mark 6 – 7
312	**November 8**	Mark 8 – 9
313	**November 9**	Mark 10 – 11

DAY	DATE	SCRIPTURE
314	**November 10**	Mark 12 – 13
315	**November 11**	Mark 14
316	**November 12**	Mark 15 – 16
317	**November 13**	Luke 1
318	**November 14**	Luke 2 – 3
319	**November 15**	Luke 4 – 5
320	**November 16**	Luke 6 – 7
321	**November 17**	Luke 8 – 9
322	**November 18**	Luke 10 – 11
323	**November 19**	Luke 12 – 13
324	**November 20**	Luke 14 – 16
325	**November 21**	Luke 17 – 18
326	**November 22**	Luke 19 – 20
327	**November 23**	Luke 21 – 22
328	**November 24**	Luke 23 – 24
329	**November 25**	Ephesians 1 – 3
330	**November 26**	Ephesians 4 – 6
331	**November 27**	Colossians; Philemon
332	**November 28**	Philippians
333	**November 29**	Acts 1 – 3
334	**November 30**	Acts 4 – 6
335	**December 1**	Acts 7 – 8
336	**December 2**	Acts 9 – 10

BIBLE READING PLANS

DAY	DATE	SCRIPTURE
337	**December 3**	Acts 11 – 13; Acts 14 – 16
339	**December 5**	Acts 17 – 19
340	**December 6**	Acts 20 – 22
341	**December 7**	Acts 23 – 25
342	**December 8**	Acts 26 – 28
343	**December 9**	1 Timothy
344	**December 10**	Titus
345	**December 11**	1 Peter
346	**December 12**	Hebrews 1 – 6
347	**December 13**	Hebrews 7 – 10
348	**December 14**	Hebrews 11 – 13
349	**December 15**	2 Timothy
350	**December 16**	2 Peter; Jude
351	**December 17**	John 1 – 2
352	**December 18**	John 3 – 4
353	**December 19**	John 5 – 6
354	**December 20**	John 7 – 8
355	**December 21**	John 9 – 10
356	**December 22**	John 11 – 12
357	**December 23**	John 13 – 15
358	**December 24**	John 16 – 18
359	**December 25**	John 19 – 21
360	**December 26**	1 John

THE HISTORICAL BIBLE IN A YEAR

DAY	DATE	SCRIPTURE
361	**December 27**	2 John; 3 John
362	**December 28**	Revelation 1 – 5
363	**December 29**	Revelation 6 – 11
364	**December 30**	Revelation 12 – 18
365	**December 31**	Revelation 19 – 22

WELCOME TO THE ADVENTURE
365
DAYS IN A ROW THROUGH THE
BIBLE IN COMMUNITY
NO APOLOGIES
NO TURNING BACK
DAILYAUDIOBIBLE.COM

Share Your Thoughts

With the Author: Your comments will be forwarded to the author when you send them to *zauthor@zondervan.com*.

With Zondervan: Submit your review of this book by writing to *zreview@zondervan.com*.

Free Online Resources at
www.zondervan.com

Zondervan AuthorTracker: Be notified whenever your favorite authors publish new books, go on tour, or post an update about what's happening in their lives at www.zondervan.com/authortracker.

Daily Bible Verses and Devotions: Enrich your life with daily Bible verses or devotions that help you start every morning focused on God. Visit www.zondervan.com/newsletters.

Free Email Publications: Sign up for newsletters on Christian living, academic resources, church ministry, fiction, children's resources, and more. Visit www.zondervan.com/newsletters.

Zondervan Bible Search: Find and compare Bible passages in a variety of translations at www.zondervanbiblesearch.com.

Other Benefits: Register to receive online benefits like coupons and special offers, or to participate in research.

ZONDERVAN®

ZONDERVAN.com/
AUTHORTRACKER
follow your favorite authors